WITH GEORGE WASHINGTON INTO THE WILDERNESS

The adventures of Robert the Hunter while he was learning to be a new American under the young chief, George Washington, when the Ohio Country was gained for the English-speaking people and Washington himself won the right to high command in war and peace

by
Edwin L. Sabin

with illustrations by
Will Thomson
portrait and map

to the
AMERICAN VOLUNTEER SOLDIER
who from the days of the "raw provincials" to the days of
the khaki "yanks" has emulated the spirit of young George
Washington in the service of his country

"I shall have the consolation of knowing that I have opened the way, when the smallness of our numbers exposed us to the attacks of a superior enemy; that I have hitherto stood the heat and brunt of the day, and escaped untouched in time of extreme danger; and that I have the thanks of my country, for the services I have rendered it."

Colonel George Washington,
November 15, 1754

Cover art: *"My Name is George Washington"*

NATAL PUBLISHING LLC
ARS LONGA, VITA BREVIS

Copyright© 2024 Natal Publishing

CONTENTS

PREFACE

This story centres upon the early frontier and military career of George Washington, introducing him as the sixteen-year-old surveyor, and closing when at the age of twenty-six he married and retired, for a time, from public service. During that period, 1748–1758 inclusive, the Ohio Country, that interior west of the Alleghany Mountains, was wrested from France. The narrative deals with the youth Washington's trip through three hundred miles of wilderness to the French forts near Lake Erie; his expedition to invest the Forks of the Ohio where the French were establishing Fort Duquesne; his service with the Braddock column; and his service under General Forbes when Fort Duquesne was taken at last. His courage as commissioner to the French at Lake Erie, his first victory, his defense of Fort Necessity, his performances upon Braddock's Field, his endurance and fine spirit, are featured. All this was the training that demonstrated his fitness for command in the War of Independence. His companion hero of the story is a boy, Robert the Hunter, son of Mary Harris the White Woman and Feather Eagle a Delaware, but adopted by Tanacharison the Half-King of the Mingos upon the Ohio. Christopher Gist, the famous chief Scarouady, George Croghan, Andrew Montour, Captain Joncaire, Captain Jack the Black Rifle, Shingis the Delaware, Pontiac, and other historic border characters figure, as well as Doctor Craik, old Lord Fairfax, Vanbraam, and others of Washington's personal confederates.

FOREWORD

George Washington did not spring into fame and success at one bound. That which he won he deserved. He is most widely known as the patriotic commander of the American armies in the War of Independence and as the wise first President of the United States. But he was chosen because of the things that he had already done.

If George Washington had not proved his character and his wisdom in his early campaigns and councils it is likely that another man would have been appointed commander-in-chief when the War of Independence opened; and indeed history might have been much changed as to names and events. Who may say? Washington, however, had an earned reputation; his work in the wilderness had verified his courage, patience, unselfishness, good sense and fine honor, and his military mettle. His companions upon the trail and the soldiers in his companies had confidence in young George Washington. The people saw that he was prepared for the greater commands.

The services that engaged him were also of deep importance. If the present United States, west of the Alleghany Mountains of Western Pennsylvania had remained French territory, the country facing the Atlantic Ocean might have remained a colony of Great Britain instead of expanding into the United States. At best, the Atlantic coast would have been a small and weak nation. When France lost the interior to England then the American colonies broadened and gained strength of mind and means until they decided to shift for themselves.

Washington at the age of twenty-five

GEORGE WASHINGTON

1732. Born about ten o'clock in the morning of February 22nd (by the calendar of those days, February 11th), upon the old Washington plantation of Wakefield bordering the Potomac River between Bridges' and Pope's Creek in Westmoreland County of the Colony of Virginia's "Northern Neck"—the peninsula formed by the Potomac and Rappahannock Rivers. Father, Augustine Washington; mother, Mary Ball Washington, second wife. The Washington family was of good English stock dating back to the Thirteenth Century, and had a long roll of scholars and valiant soldiers. George Washington's great-grandfather, John Washington, had settled here in Westmoreland County in 1657. When George was born he had two half-brothers, Lawrence and Augustine. He was followed by five brothers and sisters—Elizabeth, Samuel, John Augustine, Charles and Mildred.

1735. The family moves to another plantation at Hunting Creek, fifty miles northward up the Potomac. This plantation was called Washington, and later was named Mount Vernon.

1739. When George is seven the family moves again, this time down to Stafford along the east side of the Rappahannock River, opposite the town of Fredericksburg.

1743. George's father dies, aged forty-nine, when George is eleven. He leaves a widow and seven children: George's two elder half-brothers, Lawrence and Augustine, and the younger sister and brothers—Betty, Samuel, John Augustine and Charles. George is willed the Stafford plantation; other plantations and properties are willed to the other children. The mother is guardian.

1743–1745. George continues his schooling which first was under the direction of a church sexton, Mr. Grove, whom the boys called "Hobby," at the Stafford plantation; and next under Mr. Williams, near Wakefield where, after his father's death, George lives for a time with Augustine, its owner. By his mother he is taught religion and courtesies. From his father, a very powerful man, he inherits great strength, so that he is a leader in athletics. He is a fearless horseback-rider and is fond of hunting and fishing and playing at soldier. In mathematics he is good, in grammar and spelling and language not good; but he pays much attention to copying business forms and is neat in his papers. He likes the problems and out-door life of land surveying.

1746. At fourteen he decides to go to sea and become a merchant captain or an officer in the British Navy. But his mother opposes, and at the last moment he yields to her. He attends school kept by the Reverend James Marye, a Frenchman, in Fredericksburg.

1747. Leaving school he lives with his half-brother Lawrence upon the Mount Vernon plantation. Lawrence had married a daughter of William Fairfax of Belvoir, up-river from Mount Vernon. The Fairfax family was distinguished in England and in Virginia. At Belvoir there was also Lord Thomas Fairfax, elder brother of William Fairfax, recently arrived from London to enjoy his vast estate of 5,700,000 acres of Virginia lands. The boy George Washington is much at Belvoir, and Lord Fairfax takes a great liking for him.

1748. In March, having just turned his seventeenth year, George is appointed by Lord Fairfax to survey the immense tract of land which as yet has scarcely been explored. He sets out with only George William Fairfax, the twenty-two-year-old son of William Fairfax, and the two spend a month in the Virginia wilderness.

1749. In July, George Washington, now seventeen years of age, is appointed public surveyor of Virginia lands. This engages him through two years; he is out for weeks at a time, in all kinds of weather, and grows accustomed to hardships, woods lore and Indian ways. Between whiles he is frequently at Greenway Court, Lord Fairfax's residence seat near Winchester, Frederick County, where he studies and hunts with his old friend; he visits his brothers and his mother.

1751. At the age of nineteen he is commissioned by the Governor of Virginia as an adjutant-general, with rank of Major, in charge of a district of the Colonial Militia. His brother Lawrence, who had served with a British regiment in the West Indies and the Spanish Main, and was adjutant-general in Virginia, recommended him. This suits George. He studies military science and fencing.

1751–1752. In September of 1751 Lawrence

Washington sails for Barbadoes of the British West Indies, to gain health. George, who loves him dearly, goes with him. At Barbadoes George is stricken with the smallpox, which scars his face. He returns in the winter to Virginia, to escort his brother's wife to the Bermudas in the spring and there meet Lawrence. But Lawrence cannot wait, and comes home.

1752. This summer Lawrence dies at Mount Vernon. He wills the plantation to his little daughter, and as executor of the estate George remains there to oversee the business. Aged twenty, he is now appointed by Governor Dinwiddie of Virginia as adjutant-general of the northern military division which covers several counties.

1753. Major George Washington, aged twenty-one, is sent by Governor Dinwiddie as a commissioner to inquire into the French invasion of the Ohio River country in the northwest; for the French soldiers from Canada were building a line of forts from Lake Erie down along the Ohio River in territory claimed by Great Britain. Major Washington was to travel almost 600 miles through the wilderness, and find the French commander. He leaves Williamsburg, the Virginia capital, on the last day of October. He takes with him Christopher Gist as guide, John Davidson as Indian interpreter, Jacob Vanbraam, who had been a soldier and was a fencing master, to speak French, and four others. After a journey of forty-five days he arrives at the French headquarters post fifteen miles south of Lake Erie. On the way he notes that the "Forks of the Ohio," where the Allegheny and Monongahela Rivers join in present western Pennsylvania, is a fine site for a fort.

1754. In January Major George Washington is back to report to Governor Dinwiddie at Williamsburg that the French refuse to withdraw from their line of posts. An expedition is organized to build a British post at the Forks of the Ohio. Major Washington is commissioned lieutenant-colonel, as second in command. In April he marches with three companies to support a detachment already gone. The detachment is driven from the Forks by the French, and as commander in the field, Lieutenant-Colonel Washington entrenches at Great Meadows, short of the Forks. On May 28th he surprises a French and Indian detachment and defeats it. This is his first battle; he is twenty-two years old. Having been reinforced to 400 men, at Great Meadows he erects a log fort named Fort Necessity, in order to hold fast, and on July 3rd is attacked by 900 French and Indians. This night terms are made by which the garrison should march out with the honors of war. On July 4th Fort Necessity is abandoned to the French. The French build Fort Duquesne at the Forks of the Ohio.

1755. After the affair at Great Meadows the Colonial troops lacked men and supplies and money. Washington protests against another campaign until strength and weather permit. This spring General Edward Braddock of the British Regulars arrives to lead a force of Regulars and Colonials against Fort Duquesne. George Washington is invited to join him as aide, with rank of captain. The expedition is defeated by the French and Indians near Fort Duquesne, July 9th, in a terrible battle. General Braddock is fatally wounded, and Colonel George Washington behaves "with the greatest courage and resolution;" has two horses shot from under him and four balls through his coat.

1755–1757. Following the battle of Braddock's Field, Colonel Washington continues to live at beautiful Mount Vernon, to which he has fallen heir. He is soon appointed by the Virginia legislature to the command of all the Virginia militia. He is kept busy organizing the troops and inspecting the outposts.

1758. Having recovered from a long illness extending into March, in July he marches his Virginia regiments to take part in another expedition, this time under General Forbes, against Fort Duquesne. He leads the advance, but the fort is deserted by the enemy. The name is changed to Fort Pitt, which becomes Pittsburgh, Pennsylvania. At the close of this year Washington again retires to private life.

1759. Not quite twenty-seven years old, he is married, January 6th, to Mrs. Martha Custis, daughter of John Dandridge and widow of John Parke Custis, with two children. She is three months younger than George Washington, and wealthy in her own rights.

1759–1769. Having been elected to the Virginia House of Burgesses, or the Colonial legislature, Colonel Washington serves there. He resides at Mount Vernon, and devotes his private life to the business of his plantation, to hunting and riding, and to mingling in local society and in that of Williamsburg the capital and Annapolis the capital of Maryland. In business he is very strict, keeping full account of all transactions and shipping his tobacco to England.

1770. This fall he makes a trip, horseback, to the Forks of the Ohio again, where a few cabins around Fort Pitt mark the beginning of Pittsburgh; thence down the Ohio for 255 miles by canoe, inspecting the western lands granted to soldiers of the French and Indian War with Great Britain.

1771–1774. The American Colonies have been protesting against the Acts of the British Parliament which worked hardships upon them. In September, 1774, George Washington, aged forty-two, is a delegate from Virginia to a general Congress held at Philadelphia for the purpose of drawing up petitions of rights. Patrick Henry says that in "solid information and sound judgment" Colonel Washington was the greatest man on the floor.

1775. War with Great Britain having commenced, on June 15th the Second Continental Congress in session at Philadelphia appoints George Washington commander-in-chief of the American military forces. He takes command July 3rd, with rank of general.

1775–1782. Serves as commander-in-chief of the American army in the War of the Revolution.

1783. In October General Washington issues his Farewell Address to the army. December 4th he bids his officers goodby, in person, at Harlem, New York. December 23rd he resigns his commission, in the temporary Hall of Congress at Annapolis. December 24th he arrives home at Mount Vernon, having been absent over eight years.

1784–1786. He declines to be paid for his expenses during the war, and wishes no reward, but settles down to home and business life. His advice is much sought. He entertains many visitors, among them Lafayette; and makes a tour west to the Ohio River once more.

1787. In May he is a delegate from Virginia to the General Convention in Philadelphia to draw up a Constitution of the United States; and is chosen president of the convention.

1789. In February George Washington, aged fifty-seven, is unanimous choice of the people for first President of the United States. On March 4th the election is ratified. He is at once notified by messenger from Congress, and on March 6th he leaves Mount Vernon for New York, then the seat of Congress. He takes oath of office April 30th, and delivers his inaugural address. His mother, aged eighty-two years, dies in August. This same year he suffers a serious illness from which he never completely recovers.

1790. By his advice the present District of Columbia is selected as the site of the National Capital. He is again ill. While President he keeps close track of his plantation interests and is a student of farming methods. He looks forward to retiring to his beloved Mount Vernon.

1791. He defines the site and marks the boundaries of the new National Capital district, ten miles square, to be named Washington.

1793. The welfare of the nation demands that he remain President, and on March 4th he enters upon his second term of office.

1793–1797. Washington continues as wise and able President. In 1796 Lafayette's son, George Washington Lafayette, comes to the United States and for a year and a half is a member of Washington's household.

1797. Having declined nomination to a third term of office, and having, on September 15, 1796, issued a Farewell Address to the people of the United States, on March 4th, 1797, Washington retires from the Presidency and is succeeded by Thomas Jefferson.

1798. At Mount Vernon Washington has been following the peaceful routine of a farmer. War with France threatens, and in July he is nominated lieutenant-general and commander-in-chief of an army to be raised. He accepts and applies himself to organizing the army.

1799. December 12 he is wet and chilled with snow while riding over his land. After only twenty-four hours in bed he dies between ten and eleven o'clock at night, December 14th. December 18th he is laid to rest in the family vault at Mount Vernon. His age was sixty-seven years and ten months lacking a week.

'Tis nobly done—the day's our own—huzzah, huzzah!

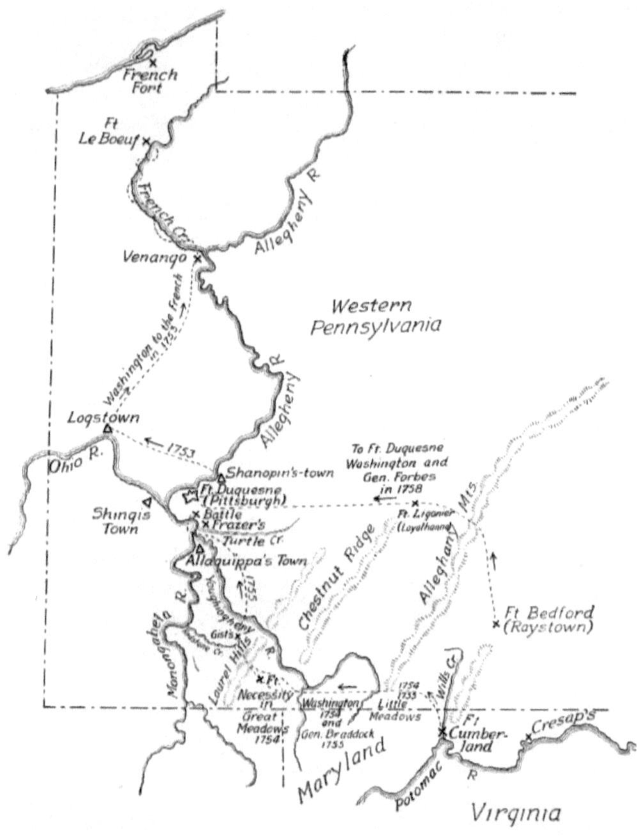

Wilderness trails of young George Washington

I

ROBERT THE HUNTER MAKES DISCOVERIES

It had been raining with a cold spring rain for two days, and the vast forest here in southern Pennsylvania of 1748 was dripping and soggy. The Indians did not mind; they were well greased with bear's grease and well painted, and their skin scarcely felt the wet. Besides, they were in a hurry.

Robert, whose Seneca name was the Hunter, did not mind it either. He also was Indian. To be sure, his mother was called the White Woman. But she had been captured forty years ago, when a little girl, by the Mohawks of the French from the north, and had been traded south, and had become the wife to Chief Feather Eagle of the Delawares in the Ohio Country.

So Robert had been brought up as an Indian boy. When his father had died the great Tan-a-char-i-son, head chief of all the Mingo Iroquois and known as Half-King, passing by White Woman's Creek on return home from a visit to the Shawnees in the west, had taken him to train him as a warrior.

To a warrior there is no weather. Heat and cold, dry and wet, they are the same to a warrior, especially a Mingo warrior of the Six Nations who have council-seats in the Long House of the proud Iroquois.

Less than a moon ago, at Logstown which was the principal village of the Mingos, upon the Ohio River, Half-King had said to Robert the Hunter:

"Listen: Tomorrow White Thunder bears a speech belt to our brothers the Delawares near the Susquehanna and I wish you to go with him. You will learn much; and if you are to be a warrior it is well that you should know your way through the woods and across the mountains."

From that Logstown upon the north bank of the upper Ohio—the Ohion-hiio or Beautiful River—seventeen or eighteen miles down from where Pittsburgh, Pennsylvania, now stands, Robert had set out with White Thunder the Keeper of the Mingo wampum belts, and with Aroas or Silver Heels the warrior, to travel afoot eastward through the forests and mountains for the Delawares of central Pennsylvania.

The Mingos were those Oneidas, Senecas and others of the Iroquois Six Nations who had moved from New York into Western Pennsylvania which the Iroquois claimed to have conquered. They thought little of the Delawares. The Iroquois had claimed to have conquered the Delawares also, and called them "women." But all the Indian peoples—Iroquois, Delawares, Shawnees, Wyandots, Miamis—had been invited to meet the English in council at Albany, the capital of New York, this coming June, to talk peace again. Therefore Half-King Tanacharison wisely wished to learn what the Delawares to the east of him were going to do.

Now this was no small journey, although, of course, it was nothing to an Indian. Nobody except Indians and birds and beasts lived in that country, and the only white persons to cross it were the traders. But the game such as bear, deer and turkeys was plentiful, and the three travellers from Logstown had meat at every camp.

Little happened during the first half of the trip. Then, on a sudden in a cloudy day, Aroas, who was leading with gun in hand, stopped short.

"Wah!" he said, to White Thunder. "This is it."

"Yes," replied White Thunder, stopping also. "This is it. It is alive?"

"Men have passed," said Silver Heels. "And not long ago."

They both studied the trail. The trail was a narrow one, wending right on amid the great trees of the silent, sunless forest. Something about the trail, and the manner with which Aroas and White Thunder held back from it struck the Hunter like a sensation of lurking death.

They two were bending forward, reading the trail. The Hunter himself could see that there were tracks in it—moccasin tracks lightly printed upon the soft soil and pressing twigs into the mud and leaves.

"Do we fear the Delaware?" he asked.

"No," answered White Thunder. "This is not their land. The land once given to them by the Iroquois has flowed through their stomachs, for they sold it to the English for rum. They wear petticoats. Here is a danger trail."

"What is that?"

"It is the Catawba Trail. Be silent."

The Catawba Trail! There was war between the Catawbas and the Pennsylvania Indians. The fierce Catawbas lived in the south, near the Cherokees. They were not many, but they sent warriors from South Carolina up through Virginia and Maryland into Ohio, Pennsylvania, and clear into New York to attack the Shawnees, the Wyandots, the Delawares and the Iroquois.

This much Robert the Hunter knew. Evidently Catawbas had passed here. He waited while Aroas and White Thunder, speaking low, discussed matters.

"Catawba moccasins. I think not many," said Aroas.

"They stepped each in the other's track, but the tracks are not deep," White Thunder agreed. "The leaves and twigs are still flat; the break in this piece of rotten wood is fresh. The Catawba passed an hour ago."

"Wah!" said Aroas. "That is good. Come."

He leaped over the trail; White Thunder leaped; and the Hunter, without asking why that was done, also leaped. Now Aroas again led through the forest, travelling rapidly so that Robert, at the end of the single file, was kept at a little trot.

All the afternoon they hurried, hurried, without speaking, through the dense forest, into ravines and out, up hill and down, until at dusk Silver Heels halted, with hand raised. He went forward alone, and bent to examine the ground. He came back.

"We are ahead," he said.

"The trail is empty?"

"Yes."

"Good!" exclaimed White Thunder. "This is the place. We will stay."

The "place" proved to be a nearby ledge of rock. It overhung at one side, making a roof; beneath the roof the ground was dry and soft with leaves blown in, and leaves were massed into a bed as though a panther or other wild animal had lain upon them.

In here they three could sit. They did sit, and munched cold deer meat and corn cake, while in the dark forest wolves began to howl and many things rustled.

Neither Silver Heels nor White Thunder made a fire, by which the Hunter understood that enemies might be near.

"Let us drink," said White Thunder. "Then sleep. We must be up before daylight." And he added, to Robert, "Follow Aroas and do as he does."

A little stream sounded not far away, in the night. Silver Heels went out, on a half circle, to the stream; and lying down drank, and the Hunter drank beside him. Ah, but that cold water was good, for they had not drunk since noon.

They met White Thunder, coming to drink. Then they rolled in their blankets, upon the leaves of the shallow cave, to sleep. But White Thunder spoke:

"The boy should know, so that he will wake and be ready for the thing that will happen."

"That is right," replied Aroas. "You should tell him about the Catawba. Some day he will fight the Catawba."

"Listen, boy," said White Thunder: "Now we sleep beside the Catawba Trail. We left the trail, and we have come to it again. First the Catawba were ahead of us; now they are behind us. Since the day of the first man and woman the Catawba and Cherokee have fought us who live in the north. This trail is the great war trail upon which the Catawba travel. I will tell you why we did not follow it, but jumped across it and went around.

"A long time ago the Catawba marched into the country of the Delaware. They found a Delaware camp. They tied buffalo hoofs to their feet and made buffalo tracks in the snow. Then in the morning the Delaware saw the buffalo tracks, and followed to hunt meat. The Catawba surprised them, and killed many and ran off with the scalps. The Delaware from the camp gave chase, for the trail was plain. But the Catawba had set sharp splinters dipped in snake poison in the trail, and the Delaware stepped on these and were made sick. Then the Catawba turned about and caught the Delaware and killed more.

"The Catawba are cunning. Their minds are full of evil tricks. To hunt the Catawba is more dangerous than hunting the panther or the mother bear. When you see a Catawba trail, be very careful of it. Now in the morning we rise early, to be ready. The Catawba are not many. They shall run home weeping."

By his snores Silver Heels was asleep before White Thunder had finished. White Thunder himself went to sleep right away. And the Hunter, with White Thunder's words in his mind, fell asleep too, and dreamed of the dread Catawba from the south.

Aroas and White Thunder were up early, when the birds were first twittering and the wolves were slinking to their dens after the night's hunt.

"Wake. You may come," said White Thunder to Robert the Hunter, shaking him by the shoulder. "It is time."

They crawled out of their own den, and climbed on top of the ledge. The top was flat and screened by low bushes. Here they lay, with the Hunter just behind.

The gloom of the forest gradually thinned. Birds began to flit. A raccoon passed, humping to his hollow tree. The dawn swiftly brightened. Squirrels chattered. Then one discovered the three persons upon the top of the ledge. He sat upon a branch and scolded angrily.

"Brother!" Aroas hissed. "Go! We mean you no harm."

The squirrel only whisked hither and thither, still scolding, so that he disturbed the forest. White Thunder spoke to Robert.

"That squirrel is a fool. He must be silenced. Shoot him."

The Hunter strung his bow and fitted an arrow to the string. Sitting up he drew and aimed; he loosed. The bow twanged, the blunt arrow streaked through the air and with a thud knocked the squirrel far.

"Wah!" uttered Aroas. "That was well done."

The sun was about to rise. Peering ahead, as Silver Heels and White Thunder were peering, Robert could see the Catawba Trail which opened clearly and crossed the stream down there in front of the ledge. Now a doe came, mincing and craning, through the trees. She did not smell them, for she paused at the stream, and drank. Suddenly she lifted her head, with long ears set forward, and sniffed. She wheeled about and away she leaped, and was gone.

"They come," whispered White Thunder to Aroas. The two cocked their muskets, and settled motionless; and behind them Robert the Hunter glued more flatly, his heart beating.

Nothing was to be heard, for a few minutes. Then around a curve of the narrow trail a warrior trotted, and another and another. The Catawbas! There were six dark, round-faced men, in red-fringed buckskin, with turkey-feathered head-dresses and with guns. This was the first time that the Hunter had seen a Catawba.

Before they arrived at the stream they stopped. They seemed to suspect the ledge as an ambush place. But Aroas gave the call of a blue-jay, as if the blue-jay were seeing the Catawbas and was giving an alarm. The jay had not cried before. The Catawbas would think they were the only strangers here. They came on.

The muskets of White Thunder and Silver Heels had been thrust forward. The first Catawba stooped, to drink at the stream, when with a terrible whoop White Thunder fired. Aroas whooped and fired. Robert the Hunter whooped and sent an arrow whizzing. All the forest echoed to the whoops and the shots, as if a dozen men had attacked; and still whooping while they reloaded in a jiffy, drawing their hatchets White Thunder and Aroas ran boldly down. But the Catawbas had vanished; the last of them could just be heard bolting through the brush up the trail. The warrior at whom White Thunder had fired lay at the edge of the stream; the warrior at whom Aroas had fired had left blood.

"Wah!" exclaimed Aroas. "Let him go."

"And we will go, too, before they stop to think," said White Thunder. So he took the scalp of the dead Catawba. Then, they hurried on, and travelled all day without a stop.

White Thunder delivered the wampum belt to the Delawares of the Susquehanna. They promised to join the Mingos in the march to the Albany council. This promise was made quickly, for the trophy of the Catawba scalp spread excitement. As soon as the Delawares learned that the Catawbas were in the country they made ready to pursue, on the war trail.

Big Bear commanded the Delawares. The Mingos were invited to join, and travel home that way. So they all set out, to see what had become of the Catawbas.

The forest seemed peaceful again. It was hard to believe that danger lurked among the trees, but the scalp at White

Thunder's belt showed what might happen at any moment.

In the second night the rain commenced; and when they wakened at daybreak they were wet and the forest was wet and soon the trails would be washed bare.

"This is bad," said Big Bear. "But we will go on and maybe the rain will stop. If it doesn't, our guns will be wet and we will be blind, and the Catawba will get away."

The rain did not stop. At noon they halted, to talk.

"I feel that somebody is following us," said Aroas, to Big Bear. "We should be careful."

"The Mingo is thinking of his wife and a lodge fire," answered Big Bear. "He hears the rain drip and it sounds to him like the feet of a Catawba. But the Delaware mean to strike the Catawba."

"Just the same," insisted Aroas, "there are enemy near. The Delaware have seen that the Mingo are not afraid, but these woods are full of evil."

And even while he was speaking a gun cracked and with a screech a Delaware warrior sprang high and fell flat. In an instant everybody had dived behind a tree. From his tree trunk the Hunter, squatting low like a partridge, listened breathlessly. A Delaware, peeking, suddenly pointed his gun, and fired—and in the same moment a gun answered him and he dropped, shot through the head. A man yelled loudly, and darted backward into the brush. Robert glimpsed him—a large man, with long black hair and dark skin, in leggins and hunting shirt and fur cap. That was not an Indian. Big Bear leaped forward, and his gun only snapped upon the flint, for the priming was wet.

He stopped and ducked just in time; a bullet must have sped over him. Now the Delawares were crying—"The Black Rifle! It is death! Run!" Run they did, Big Bear the same as the others, and the Mingos and Robert following.

They ran helter skelter, much as the Catawbas had run when surprised. At last they stopped, and gathered again.

"You said truly, brother," Big Bear panted, to Aroas. "The Black Rifle was upon our trail. Now we have lost two warriors. Wah! But he is not a man; he is a demon."

"We have heard of the Black Hunter," said White Thunder. "He is like death on the trail of the Indian. He strikes to kill, like the wounded bear. The Delaware have lost many warriors to the Black Hunter of the Juniata."

And Robert himself had heard of Captain Jack, the giant settler who roamed the Pennsylvania woods, killing Indians in revenge for his family whom Indians had killed. The "Black Rifle" and the "Black Hunter" were the names given him. He feared nothing, no bullet could hurt him; he always struck before he was seen. It was small wonder that the Delawares ran to save their lives.

"The way home is closed," Big Bear was saying. "But there will be English in the south, and blood shall pay for blood."

"No. Your talk is wild talk," White Thunder opposed. "You will do foolish to go against the English, and break the chain of friendship."

"The Black Rifle is English, and two fresh Delaware scalps are hanging at his belt," Big Bear retorted. "Why should we not kill the English?"

"The Black Rifle did it; not the English. He is a mad dog. The English are friends of the Mingo. They are welcome at Logstown. They will help us against the French who claim the country of the Ohio."

"The English are driving the Delaware from the land granted them by the first father called Penn," Big Bear answered. "Soon there will be only the Ohio Country in the west for the Delaware. The Delaware would rather have the French. The French do not take land; they give it. The English build forts and houses and clear off the land and there is no game, no place for the Indian. They shoot us. They call the Indians, dogs. The French leave things as they are; they ask the Indian to live near and hunt; they call the Indian, brother."

"The friendship chain between the English and the Six Nations is strong," said White Thunder. "The men of Onontio (which was the name for the French governor of Canada) are not wanted on the Ohio. The English bring us goods and that is enough."

"We hear that the English claim all the land on one side of the Ohio and the French claim all the land on the other side," replied Big Bear. "Then where does the Indian's land lie? But seeing you will not strike the English with us, we will all go on to the trading house of the Englishman Cresap on the River Potomac. He will give us presents and fire-water to keep out the wet."

That was all right. The Delawares and the Mingos with Robert the Hunter marched on through the rain. The Black Rifle and the rain had spoiled the war trail and the hearts of the Delawares were heavy.

The law of the forest seemed to be tit for tat. The Indians killed other Indians and white persons; the white men killed Indians. As to the French, Robert knew little, except he had heard that the French, who lived in the north, would shut the English traders from the Ohio Country.

They hastened southward, and the next noon a scout came back with word that he had seen a company of English. In these years before the War of the Revolution all the white men of the Colonies were English to the Indian, for America was a British province.

"How many?" asked Big Bear.

"The fingers of two hands."

"What are they doing?"

"They are camped in the rain above the house of the Englishman Cresap."

"Our guns are wet," Big Bear said. "It is a bad time to fight. Let us go in to them. We will tell them we are poor and they will give us food and drink."

They went on. The rain stopped. In the middle of the afternoon they sighted the Englishmen's camp in a clearing of the forest upon the north bank of the upper Potomac of northern Maryland.

Then they whooped the scalp whoop and ran in. The English were eight Long Knives of Virginia, and stayed firm. Trader Cresap was here; two of the others were young; and when Big Bear asked who was the captain, Trader Cresap pointed to the younger of the two.

This captain appeared to be few in years, but was large and well formed, and had the grave air of a chief.

"Wah! A boy!" White Thunder grunted.

Big Bear shook hands with the boy, intending to grip him hard and make him cry out, which was an Indian joke. Instead it was Big Bear who cried out, astonished, for the young

Englishman had gripped him first and had squeezed his hand so that the bones were almost crushed.

"Ugh!" Big Bear exclaimed. "A strong boy. As strong as a man."

After they had shown the Catawba scalp and had received presents, Big Bear ordered a war dance, to celebrate the scalp. They built a large fire and all sat around while Big Bear made a speech, telling of the deeds of the Delawares and of the love they had for the English. Then the dance began, and so did the music. One warrior thumped a deer hide stretched tightly over a pot half full of water; and another shook a rattle, of a dry gourd with shot inside it and a horse tail tied to it. The other Delawares, and Silver Heels, pranced around the fire, whooping.

White Thunder and Robert the Hunter looked on, with the English. The English, especially the young captain, were much pleased, for it was a fine dance.

After a time the young captain moved and sat beside White Thunder and Robert, as if curious to ask questions. The friend whom he had left was slender and tall and handsome, in three-cornered hat and red wool blanket-coat and decorated leather belt and deerskin trousers and knee boots. His name was Fairfax. The young captain himself was not so handsome; but he had steady blue eyes and large, straight nose, and a kind, but sober face tanned brown; and he was as heavy and as muscular as White Thunder.

He wore three-cornered hat, deer-hide shirt and cloth trousers and moccasins. Like his friend he was very different from the English traders who came with pack horse and canoe to Logstown of the Mingos.

He kept glancing at Robert. What he saw was a hard, wiry boy, in beaded hunting-shirt and leggins and moccasins, with bow and otter-skin quiver, and black eyes and long brown hair and skin as brown as an Indian's, and both cheeks painted with a red dot in a blue circle—a Mingo sign that Robert thought very becoming.

"Your boy?" the young captain asked of White Thunder.

And White Thunder, the Keeper of Wampum, who spoke English, said:

"No. Belong Tanacharison, Half-King."

"Delaware?"

"No! Seneca. No Delaware. Seneca."

"Where are you from?"

"Shenango, what English call Logstown, 'way off beyond mountains, on Beautiful River."

"The Ohio?"

"Yes. What you do here?"

"We make lands," said the young captain.

"Injun lands?"

"No. English lands."

"You walk heap 'round?" For that had been the way: to take as much land as one could walk around in a day, and the Indians had lost much land because the white men had cleared a path beforehand and had sent their fastest walkers.

"No," the young chief answered. "We measure with a steel rope and spy-glass. I am a surveyor."

"Humph!" said White Thunder. "Pretty soon mebbe you come with spy-glass to make English lands of Injun lands other side mountains."

"That too is the country of the great king across the water," answered the young captain. And he asked of Robert, very gravely: "You are Indian?"

"His father Injun, he Injun," said White Thunder. "Some day he great warrior."

"What is your name?"

"The Hunter," said Robert.

"You're not all Indian. You have white boy's hair."

"My mother called the White Woman. But me Injun; Seneca. My father Tanacharison, Half-King. He chief of all the Mingo," Robert asserted proudly. His father really was not Tanacharison. Tanacharison had only adopted him, but there was no use in saying that.

"Where does your mother live?"

"White Woman Creek, in Shawnee country. I live Logstown with Half-King. Learn to be warrior; then follow war trail."

"Against the English?"

"No. English are brothers of the Mingo."

"Are the French not brothers?"

"No," said Robert the Hunter. "Do not want French."

"There are English in Logstown?"

"Many. Traders."

"How old are you?"

"Ten summers."

"I am sixteen," said the young English captain. "My name is George Washington. Perhaps someday I will be a warrior."

"You come to your brothers the Mingo?" proposed Robert.

"Maybe I shall," agreed George Washington. "Wouldn't you like to stay here and be English?"

"No," said Robert. "Me Seneca."

And it seemed to him that to be a Seneca was the best thing in the world, for the Senecas were of the Six Nations and had a council seat in the Long House of the Iroquois. But if the English were like this young chief they were not so bad, either.

The dance was slackening. The young captain moved away to his companions. After the dance the Indians ate and drank again, and made camp in the dusk.

The next day the English broke camp, and marched up river, to cross over. The Indians followed, to watch and to get last presents. George Washington waded far out, driving his horse before him, to swim it. The current tugged at him, and Robert the Hunter brought him a large rock.

"Carry this, to keep feet down," he said to George Washington. "That Injun way."

George Washington thanked him politely, and carried the rock. Thus a Seneca boy had showed a white boy what an Indian could do better.

The English all crossed. The Delawares went on, and the Mingos turned for home. And this was the first meeting of Robert the Hunter, whose mother was Mary Harris of White Woman Creek, and of George Washington, the surveyor. But they were to meet again.

"He is a strong young man," said White Thunder, speaking of Washington. "He will be a chief. He is now marking off lands for the English to live on. Some day he will mark off lands clear to the Ohio. The English will live there, the Injuns will live on the other side, and there will be no place for the French. That is good. When white men fight over Injun land the Injun gets the blows."

They travelled rapidly into the west; and in due time were at Logstown, where Tanacharison the Half-King heard from White Thunder and from Robert of their adventures.

"What you say of this Washington sounds well," he uttered, to the Hunter, that night. "But he is only a boy, and so are you. When he grows to a warrior, then let him come to Logstown. Meanwhile the English should send a captain chief with men and big guns to build a great house on the Ohio so that we may trade with them and not be bothered by the French."

"Why should the French try to drive out the English?" Robert asked.

"Because they also wish the Indian furs. And they wish the Beautiful River and all the land that it waters, from the Great Lakes to the big water south of the home of the Creeks."

"Did they conquer it?" asked Robert.

"No, the Iroquois have conquered it by conquering the people. The French say that a captain of theirs, many years ago, discovered it by floating down the River Mississippi in the west, in a canoe. He took it for the King of France. But the Indians owned it; they were here first; the French have not conquered the Indians. The Iroquois are the conquerors, and they say that their brothers the English shall trade in this land and that their enemies the French shall stay out. The French have their own country. The Indians and the English have theirs. We are children of the British father, who treats us well. We cannot share our lands with two white nations or pretty soon we shall have nothing. I am telling you these things so that you may understand, and not listen to the foolish words of the Delawares."

Robert continued to think a great deal about that other boy, George Washington, who asked questions like a boy but acted like a man. If the Long Knife and the Pennsylvania boys were that kind of a boy, so strong and steady, the English beyond the mountains were going to be very powerful when the boys grew up.

George Croghan the trader, and Andrew Montour who

spoke for Onas the governor of Pennsylvania, and gay Captain Joncaire of the French, were fine men; but somehow George Washington was different, like a young eagle among hawks, or a young oak in a clearing.

II
ALARM AT LOGSTOWN

Logstown, or Shenango, the head village of the Mingos, was nicely located in a clearing of the forest upon the high north bank of the Ohio River, a half day's travel below De-ka-na-wi-da—the two-rivers-flowing-together place. This place, where the Monongahela River from the southward and the Allegheny River from the northward joined to form the Ohio or Beautiful River, the English traders called the Forks.

Logstown contained some fifty log cabins and skin and bark lodges and almost three hundred people. Fifteen miles east up the Ohio, on the south bank near the Forks, there was the Delaware village of fiery old King Shingis, sachem of the Delawares. On the Monongahela south of the Forks there was the village of fat old Queen Allaquippa, a woman sachem of the Delawares. Up the Allegheny, on the east bank just north of the Forks there was the village Shanopin's-town of old King Shanopin, another Delaware sachem. And further north up the Allegheny there was Kittanning, where more Mingos and Delawares lived under command of the Delaware chief named Captain Jacobs.

West from Logstown, down along the Ohio by the Shawnee Trail there were the Delawares of King Beaver, and the Wyandots or Little Mingos of Muskingum, and the Shawnees and Delawares of White Woman's Creek which was the home of Robert's mother, and the Shawnees of Sonnioto or Scioto.

All, all this country of the Ohio River was Indian country. But to Robert the Hunter the Logstown of the Mingos was the most important place. He rather doubted whether the Englishmen's Albany or Philadelphia could equal it.

Tanacharison was the chief man in Logstown. He was about fifty years old, and wise. The Grand Council of the Six Nations, sitting at Onondaga, New York, had appointed him head of the Mingos of the Ohio River country, therefore he ranked as a Half-King among the Iroquois.

Next to him there was Scarouady, or Beyond-the-sky, a chief and orator of the Oneida Mingos. In the Delaware tongue his name was Mona-cath-u-atha, which was the name given to the Half-King also; but he was better known as Scarouady. The English traders called him "Scaddy."

Anybody who looked upon Scarouady saw a warrior and chief indeed. He was over six feet tall, and straight and sinewy and active. Already he had fought in more than twenty-five battles, so that his leggins and his hunting shirt were fringed with scalp hair. His head was shaven except for the long braided scalp lock, to be taken by the hand that could take it; the chief's sign, a tail plume of the bald eagle, was thrust through the base of the scalp lock, and the braid was decorated with blue-jay feathers.

Upon his broad chest a tomahawk—the warrior sign— had been tattooed in blue; and the hunter sign, of bow and arrow, had been tattooed upon either cheek.

With his light coppery skin, his high forehead, a large, straight nose set between his wide cheek bones, his black eyes and his firm, thin lips, this was the brave Scarouady, friend to the English and to Robert the Hunter.

Then there was White Thunder or Belt of Wampum, who had a pretty daughter named Bright Lightning; and old Juskakaka or Green Grasshopper, whom the English called "Little Billy;" and Guyasuta or Standing Cross, a famous young warrior; and Aroas or Silver Heels, another Seneca warrior; and other valiant men, all of whom regarded Tanacharison and Scarouady as their leaders.

Here to Logstown came the English traders: John Fraser on his way to his trading house in the Seneca and Delaware town of Venango, sixty miles northward, where he stored his goods and made guns to sell; and John Davidson of the Virginia Long Knives, and Captain George Croghan of Pennsylvania of the east; and others, driving their pack horses over the mountains and crossing the river in wooden canoes, to stay at Logstown and to trade beads, paint, powder, lead, blankets and rum for furs.

And here came Captain Andrew Montour, who was part Huron and part Seneca and part white, to talk for the Governor of Pennsylvania; and once in a long time the merry

Captain Joncaire, half Seneca, from the French of Canada. These two were gaily dressed, and spoke the Iroquois tongue, and were accounted great men.

So that with the Indians in paint, blankets and moccasins, and the traders in whiskers, fur caps and deer-hide shirts, and speech makers like Captains Montour and Joncaire, and the women, children and dogs, Logstown beside the broad, blue Ohio flowing amid forest and meadow, rich in deer, bear and wild turkey, was a stirring town.

Now this summer Juskakaka and White Thunder with speech belts were sent to the council to be held with the English at Albany of New York in the country of the Iroquois council fire.

When they two returned they reported that the French of Canada were getting ready to seize the Ohio River. The Iroquois spies were certain of this, and so were the English.

The Six Nations League of the Iroquois were friends of the English, and enemies of the French. That had long been the case. All the Iroquois lands from the Alleghany Mountains to the setting sun were open to the English; "for," said the Iroquois, "we have conquered it, and it is yours who are our brothers."

Therefore, at the big council, the Iroquois agreed to help the English to keep the French out. The English were to put many more traders into the Ohio River country, so that the Indians should be fat with goods and strong to fight.

The Mingos had been directed to talk with the Delawares and the Shawnees, and ask them to take up the hatchet against the French, and against the Ottawas and the Potawatomis of the north, who were allies of the French. But the Delawares and Shawnees of the Ohio were undecided.

King Shingis of the Delawares spoke fiercely. He was a small man, but strong and quick, and his eyes glowed hotly. He hated the English, and wished no white men at all.

"No," he said. "This is our country. The Delaware are men. They stand on their own ground. If the French and English desire to fight, let them fight in their own land or on the big water. If they fight here, the Indian will be like cloth under a pair of shears and will be cut in pieces. We ask for nothing but to be let alone. Besides, the English are stingy.

They give little. The French give much. The Swannoks (which was a name of contempt for the English) fool us with trash and take our lands and drive us out. The French will leave us our lands and live among us."

And so said King Beaver, of the Delawares farther west, in Ohio.

"The Delaware are not women, to be ordered by the Iroquois," said King Beaver. "Three times the Iroquois have sold our lands and made us move. Now this is our land and not a Frenchman nor an Englishman shall have one foot of it."

And so said Killbuck, and Kateuskund. Old Shanopin of Shanopin's-town said nothing; but the fiery young Cat-a-he-cassa or Blackhoof of the Shawnees cried angrily:

"What our grandfathers the Delaware say, we say. Onontio is a better man than the King of the Swannoks, but we wish no white men except traders in our land."

The French came. Runners from the Senecas of Venango in the north panted in to declare that the French of Onontio were descending the Allegheny River in twenty-three canoes. There were more than two hundred soldiers and Ottawas under a French captain; and they were sending Captain Joncaire the half-Seneca ahead, to make things ready. They were burying lead plates and nailing up signs at the mouths of the rivers, seizing the land for Onontio, and driving out the English traders.

"The English have not yet come to help us," said Tanacharison, in the Mingo council. "They should have built a fort with great guns in it, to turn the French back. Let us hear what these French have to say. To show that we are not at war we will put up the flags of the two nations."

So the King George's red flag given by the English traders was kept up, and the white French flag sent last year by Captain Joncaire himself was put up. Soon Indians from the outside again hurried in. Delawares of Kittanning up the Allegheny arrived to say that the French had landed there and had found nobody; and the Shawnees and Delawares from Shanopin's-town arrived to say that the French had passed there; and Mingos and Delawares from fat Queen Allaquippa's town of the Monongahela south of the Forks arrived to say that the French were there.

And the next noon here came, in a canoe paddled by Ottawas but bearing no soldiers, Captain Joncaire, bringing another French flag.

A swarthy, wrinkled man, was Captain Joncaire; small, lean, quick, dark but gray-haired, constantly smiling and merry, but exceedingly sharp. It was only by his smiles and his white teeth that he showed his French blood. His father was a French officer of Canada, but his mother was a Seneca and he spoke the Seneca tongue.

Now wearing a blue French soldier coat with captain's epaulets, and gaily beaded leggins and moccasins, and a woodsman's cap on his long gray hair, and a sword at his belt and a rifle on his back he sprang ashore at Logstown.

"Greetings to my brothers," he called, in Seneca. "I am come from your father Onontio. A greater one than I am is following with presents and important words. Am I welcome?"

But he was answered with murmurs and black looks. With his Ottawas of the French he strode on to the council house where Tanacharison would be waiting for him. He and the chiefs smoked the calumet pipe; then Tanacharison the Half-King asked:

"What does my brother wish in Shenango?"

"I am come alone," said Captain Joncaire. "I am a Seneca, I am among brothers. I come from the French of Onontio, who also are my brothers. The great Onontio does not like to see two flags floating in this country which he shares with his red children. He has heard that the English are crossing the mountains into your country and his, and are poisoning the minds of his children. So he is sending a company under a mighty captain down the Beautiful River to talk with his children the Mingo, the Wyandot, the Delaware, the Shawnee. From Shenango the captain goes on to scourge home the Miami and the Wyandot further west who have listened to the false songs of the English. This is French country; our father Onontio wishes all the Indians to live here at peace, but he will have no English traders, who are only spies."

"Is Onontio at war with the English king across the

water?" Half-King asked.

"He is not at war, but his arm is long; it can reach across the water," said Captain Joncaire. "You know me as your brother. I live in your houses. I tell you the truth. You cannot think to stand still and be the children of the French and of the English both. That is impossible. The English seek to drive you from your lands; the French seek to hold your lands for you. Have the French ever stolen land from under your feet? No! But with the French pulling you one way and the English pushing you another, you will be torn in two. So now the French are coming in to hold you on the land, and the English must get out. They have no right between the mountains and the setting sun."

"We will talk with the captain sent by Onontio," said Tanacharison.

When the warriors knew what had been said in the council, Logstown was much excited. Those Indians who wanted no whites at all were in favor of killing the ten English traders in town and not letting the French land. Tanacharison sent the Hunter to tell the traders to be careful and to stay indoors. Those Indians who wished the English were also in favor of not letting the French land and bury plates that would make the country French. The Mingos were for obeying the words of Tanacharison, and hearing what the captain sent by Onontio had to say, under the peace flag. So between the warriors of Tanacharison, helped by Scarouady and White Thunder, and the Delawares and Shawnees of Shingis and Blackhoof, there was hot talk.

In mid-afternoon the fleet of canoes swept into the bend and bore down for Logstown. The paddles flashed, guns glistened, and the white flag with the golden lilies of France streamed in the breeze from the foremost boat.

Everybody rushed to the high bank, where the canoe landing was. The muskets and rifles volleyed—Bang! Bang! Crack! Crack!—in salute and in warning, too, for the bullets splashed the canoes with water.

The canoes, crowded with the sky-blue coats and the white breeches of the soldiery, almost stopped; but the French captain bravely stood up and shouted, in French:

"What is this? Do you fire on your brothers from

Onontio? Quit this foolishness or we will give you ball for ball."

Tanacharison and Scarouady and Captain Joncaire struck aside the barrels of the guns, and the warriors ceased firing. The French came on; they climbed the bank and marched to a piece of higher ground above the town, nearer the forest, and made camp.

They placed guards around their camp; the head captain sent word to the chiefs that he wished to meet them in council; and Half-King replied that he must wait until the chiefs had talked together.

It was another stormy talk. Shingis and Blackhoof were still for war; they would drive off the French and the English both, and many of the Mingos were for wiping out these French anyway. But the French were strong and well guarded in their camp, and Captain Joncaire had friends who would tell him what was being planned. So although the town was in a hubbub through most of the night, nothing was done, and in the morning the council with the French captain, whose name was Céleron, sat to hear what he would say.

Captain Joncaire translated. The French captain, standing up in his best uniform, said:

"Onontio your father speaks to you with these words: Through the love I bear you, my children, I send to you Captain de Céleron to open your eyes to the schemes of the English against your lands. What they mean to do will ruin you. They work in secret, but they plan to build houses upon your lands and settle here and drive you away, if I let them. As a good father who loves his children and far away keeps them always in his heart I warn you of the danger that threatens you. The English plan to rob you of your country, and first they rob you of your minds. They mean to seize the Ohio which belongs to me; so I have ordered Captain de Céleron to tell them to go out, and leave Shenango and all other villages of my children of the Ohio."

Then Tanacharison answered:

"Our brother from Onontio sees us poor. We are a long way from Onontio. The goods he sends us are many moons getting here. That our wives and children may not go cold and hungry we trade with the English, who are always with us.

We ask Onontio to let us trade a little while yet with the English who have come. They are our guests and it is not right to put them out. We understand that you are burying lead plates and nailing up signs to claim this land. We do not know why this is French land. The English say that it is English land. Where is the Indian land? We are made poor; and if we do not get goods from the English we will starve."

This was a clever speech, which promised nothing. Then the French captain stood again, and said:

"By the gifts that your father sends you he promises to take care of his children. Stand firm against the English, and soon your father will raise a barrier against them and the sky will always be calm over your heads. This shall be your land to enjoy as you please, if you remain true children. As for these English now here, I myself will order them to go back to their own country."

That he did, after the council. The ten traders agreed to leave, and the French went on down the Beautiful River, to talk with the Wyandots, the Shawnees and the Miamis in the west. But the English traders stayed.

Now Logstown was of several minds again. Old King Shingis was satisfied.

"The English are being driven out," he said. "That is good. The French speak fair words, and we shall see whether they lie or not. If they think to settle here, we will drive them out, too, for this is Indian land. Then we will be rid of all whites."

George Croghan, who was a great trader from Pennsylvania and had a store-house in Logstown, came to Tanacharison and said:

"Listen, brother. This is the country of your father Onas." Onas was the name for the governor of Pennsylvania. "Pay no attention to the twitters of the French, for we pay no attention to them. The French are far, but Onas is near. He it is who sends us over the mountains to trade with you, and our goods are cheap. But these Virginia men plan to settle upon your country and you should watch them, or they will try to buy you with their goods."

Everybody· knew that there was rivalry between the Pennsylvania traders and the Virginia traders. The traders of

Onas claimed the right to trade, for they said that the Forks of the Ohio and the country near were Pennsylvania. The Virginians said it all was Virginia.

So Tanacharison went to John Davidson, of the Virginia traders, and said:

"Is it true that Assaragoa (which was the name for the Governor of Virginia) plans to build houses and settle the Indian country?"

John Davidson replied:

"It is true that Assaragoa governs all this country from the mountains to the river, and his traders have the right to trade with you. I think the men from Onas have been talking to you. It is true, too, that your Virginia father is going to send men in to clear land and build a house on this side of the mountains, near the Ohio, and keep the French out. Then the Indians may live in peace."

"Who will bring these men in?" asked Tanacharison.

"It is a company under a man named Washington," said John Davidson.

"That is good," said Tanacharison. "I have heard of Washington, but do not know him. He is not a chief."

"He is a soldier captain and a chief," replied John Davidson.

"We shall see," said Half-King. "When you go back you tell our Virginia father to send men and build a house with guns, for the men of Onas do not say they will build houses."

Another thing happened right after the council. Robert the Hunter saw Bright Lightning, White Thunder's pretty daughter, beckon to him, and he went to her.

"I found something," said Bright Lightning. "What shall I do with it? I am afraid of it."

She showed it to him, where she had hidden it under some leaves. It was one of the lead plates brought by the French.

"Where did you get it?"

"From Captain Joncaire. He was playing with me, and when he wasn't looking I took it. There were others; so I put this under my blanket, and he didn't know. But I'm afraid of it, Hunter. It has evil signs on it. You are part white. Is this white man's witchcraft?"

The plate was marked with strange signs that Robert could not read. In fact, he could not read print, anyway—he never had learned. His reading was of signs left by animals and birds and men, upon the ground. So whether these signs were writing in French or English he did not know. They looked like witchcraft.

"We'll take it to Tanacharison," he said. "Tanacharison is wise. Maybe it ought to be burned."

They took it to Tanacharison, and Tanacharison examined it. He could make nothing of it, and none of the English could make anything of it—for the very good reason that it was written in French. Evidently this plate was a mischief plate.

"Let us send it to the head council at Onondago," said Tanacharison. "They will show it to wise English who will read it, and then we will know the designs of the French from Onontio."

White Thunder set off with the plate carefully wrapped in deer skin, for Onondago of New York.

When he returned he reported that Colonel William Johnson, the great white Mohawk brother in the Six Nations, had read the plate. The words on the plate were very bad; wherever these plates were buried they would blast the land and the Indians would sicken and die. He advised his brothers of the Ohio to have nothing whatever to do with the French.

III

The Mingos Send For Help

It was the hunting season again—the month of Fat Deer, when the leaves were beginning to fall and the flies had been killed by the first frost. No more French had been seen, but no English had come yet to build a fort.

The Mingos, the Delawares and Shawnees of Logstown were getting ready to start out on the hunt and kill meat for winter. Soon there would be only a few old persons left in Logstown. But Tanacharison spoke to Robert.

"We have been waiting for the English and their house. The trader Davidson said that Virginia was sending in men to clear land and build a house. I do not see them. You know this Washington, who makes lands. He should be getting near. Do you go with Scarouady and point him out, that we may tell him to hurry. I will show him a good place for a house with great guns."

Now that was better than a regular hunt. Robert set out gladly enough, with Scarouady the famous warrior, his good friend. He had his ash bow, powder horn and bullet pouch, his tomahawk and hunting knife; Scarouady had his English rifle, his powder horn and bullet pouch, his tomahawk and knife. With flint and steel and with a blanket each they needed nothing else, although the settlements of the English were two hundred miles through the mountains and the forests, in the east and south.

They took the Shawnee Trail up to the Forks, and crossed in a canoe that Scarouady knew of. Then following game trails they struck off for Virginia, their eyes glancing sharply right and left and down before, that nothing should be missed. No one could say what the trees and bushes might conceal.

They had been out two days and nights, when on coming to another hill Scarouady said:

"Do you go round this side and I will go round that side, and we will meet. I think we will get a deer or turkey for camp tonight."

This meant a half circle of ten or twelve miles, but that

mattered little to a hunter and warrior. The time was afternoon; the forest lay silent, beautiful and wild, with the shadows from the sun stretching long across the grassy openings, and the air sweet with the drying leaves.

His bow strung and his arrows loose in his quiver Robert trotted upon straight-footed moccasins around the hill, and through the timber and whenever he sighted a little opening he paused, to spy, in hope of seeing deer or turkey.

The way was not smooth, of course. This was virgin forest, cut by ravines and cumbered with great fallen trees that made a boy seem very small. He had traveled almost half around the hill, and was expecting to meet Scarouady any moment, or at least hear from him, when he stopped, frozen.

The route he was taking had been crossed by fresh moccasin prints, heading toward where Scarouady should be.

Robert studied the prints in the leafy mould. They were not plain enough to read; they might be Delaware, might be Mingo, might be Ottawa, and might be enemy moccasins. At any rate his business was to follow them until he found Scarouady, or else where they were going, and what the owners were doing.

So he looked and listened, and he took after the moccasins, as if he were a dog trailing. The trail led on and on, winding among the giant trees and skirting the parks. He kept his ears open and his eyes fixed, with little darts side to side; and the trail was so fresh that it made his heart thump. Something told him that these were stranger moccasins. Where was Scarouady?

Then an Indian leaped at him from behind a tree.

Robert was quick. This was no Scarouady, and was no joke. Even as he ducked and leaped, himself, and the Indian crashed by, he glimpsed a bushy head and black and yellow paint, and he knew that the Indian was from the south—likely a Cherokee or Catawba again. And away he ran, like a rabbit, full speed into the forest, with the Indian hard after.

Robert the Hunter was swift, but the Indian was swift, too. Whenever the Hunter looked behind he saw the fellow coming, with great bounds, his tomahawk raised and a grin on his painted face. He was a slender, light-skinned man, with thick hair. Yes, it was a Cherokee, and a warrior. He did not shoot, or throw his tomahawk; evidently he wished to catch this boy alive.

The Hunter had no notion of being caught and carried south. He did not take the time to fit an arrow to his bow; that would be later when he was winded and had turned at bay behind a tree of his own. He simply ran, with the Cherokee in close pursuit. His throat grew dry, and his breath grew short as he doubled and dodged, but he could not shake the Cherokee off.

It was a hot race. Robert looked behind again. The long-legged Cherokee had gained on him. They had run a mile, as it seemed to Robert. Now another fallen tree trunk barred his way. He gave a leap and a scramble, and landed plump into a growling furry body, which whirled upon him, while smaller bodies scampered right and left.

He ducked back just in time. This was a mother bear with two late cubs, half grown. And she barred the way. The Cherokee was coming. The mother bear, bristling, sniffed at Robert, then sniffed the air beyond him, and the Cherokee could be heard. Then the Hunter chuckled, and crouched low, under the log. He was to see some fun. The mother bear paid little attention to him, for he was quiet; but just as the Cherokee sprang through the screen of branches above the log she rose, and his great leap landed him into her arms.

Wah! What a noise, of bear and Cherokee language and of threshing and wrestling! The Cherokee stabbed with the knife, the mother bear bit and struck; and Robert crawled away and ran again, laughing.

Hark! That was a rifle report—Scarouady's rifle ringing among the trees. The Hunter well knew the sharp bark of Scarouady's gun. When that gun spoke, it signaled either meat or scalp. He paid no more attention to the bear-and-man fight, but ran for the place from which Scarouady's rifle had sounded.

As he ran he fitted an arrow to his bow-string. The rifle had sounded near. Now he heard the rifle again, and the scalp yell of the Mingo—a long, shrill yell, the Indian hurrah! Next he had arrived at a little dip in the forest, where the glade opened to thinner trees and low brush. Guns banged, but not at him. Just before him were several Indians, hiding behind trees, and firing and whooping; and across, from behind a log, upon which lay a dead Indian, a long rifle barrel was thrust out, between branches, threatening these nearer Indians.

The dead Indian had been scalped. Behind that rifle barrel was Scarouady. By their paint and head-dresses, these nearer Indians were Cherokees; and Scarouady was in a tight place. He could not run back to the forest; he would soon be surrounded.

The Hunter knew what to do. He gave the Mingo war whoop, and drawing the arrow to the head he let fly. A Cherokee yelped and leaped, with the arrow jutting from his left arm. Robert whooped again, his bow twanged, the arrow hissed and quivered in a tree, for attacked from the rear the four Cherokees had bolted away into the forest as if they thought that a whole company of Mingos were upon them.

Scarouady sprang up and threw his hatchet after. He whooped with triumph, and then he laughed.

"Is that you, Hunter?"

"Yes."

"Good. They are gone." He came over, with the scalp in his belt. "You did well, Hunter. You are a warrior," he said. "Wah! You have been running far."

"A Cherokee chased me; then I heard you shoot."

"Where is he?"

"I left him with a bear," said Robert; and explained.

"Ho, ho," laughed Scarouady. "We will go and see."

So he picked up his hatchet, and they back-tracked, and found the bear place. But no bear was here, and no Cherokee. The ground was torn and bloody. The bear might be dead, somewhere; and the Cherokee might be badly hurt, somewhere. Anyway, both had had enough, according to the signs.

"That was a smart trick, Hunter," Scarouady praised. "After this you must not kill a bear. The bear is good to you. Wah! The Cherokees will go home lacking one man, maybe two. They thought to strike the Delaware. Instead, they met the Mingo. Scarouady saw them. A man and a boy drove them like deer. I have hidden a turkey that I killed with my hatchet. We have a scalp. We will go on and find Washington."

They travelled on, and camped that evening, and

travelled again the next day.

"Where does this Washington live?" Scarouady asked.

"I don't know," answered Robert. "He was at the River Potomac, marking English lands."

"Such a man will be known to others," said Scarouady. "We are getting near the Potomac. See? The English have been here. They have marked the trees with hatchets. We will follow the hatchet marks and come to somebody."

The hatchet marks were new, marking a line along an old buffalo trail that seemed to lead between the Potomac and the Monongahela in the west.

"There will be English at the other end," said Scarouady. "Maybe Washington himself. He is marking lands still."

When they caught up with the tree markers, at a noon camp in the forest beside a stream, there were two of them; one was an Indian and the other was the trader Cresap.

That, however, was good. Scarouady knew the Indian, and Cresap knew Washington.

Scarouady advanced straightway, and spoke:

"Hello, Nemacolin. Hello, brother."

"Hello, Monacathuatha," replied Nemacolin, in the Delaware. He was a Delaware who lived at the Monongahela above Queen Allaquippa's town. "My brother is welcome."

"Good," said Scarouady. "What does my brother do here, far from home and his hunting ground, marking trees with a white man?"

"We make a road for an English company to travel over from the Potomac to the Monongahela," said Nemacolin. "The English are blind, so I show this man the way, for it is my road through the Little Meadows and the Great Meadows and over the Laurel Hills to the Monongahela."

"Wah!" exclaimed Scarouady. "An English company? That is the Washington company?"

"I do not know," replied Nemacolin. "It is an English company to build a great house on my land and keep many goods there."

"Wah!" again exclaimed Scarouady. "The Washington company. Who is this white man?"

"He is named Cresap. He lives in the east, down the river Potomac."

"Wah!" said Scarouady. And he bade of Robert: "Ask that man where we find the young captain, Washington."

"He will know," Robert said eagerly. "It was at his place that I saw Washington." So he said, in English: "We look for Washington."

The Englishman, who was burly and bearded, smiled.

"It is you, is it, young man? You want to see George Washington again?"

"We come to find Washington," Robert the Hunter repeated. "At your place?"

"No, George Washington doesn't live at my place. That was a long time ago. You travel east, down the Potomac, to Will's Creek. Ask at the Ohio Company's house there, and they'll tell you where to find George Washington. He's likely down south at Greenway Court, near the Shenandoah, on the Lord Fairfax plantation. Or else in the woods, surveying. Understand?"

Much of this was Greek to Robert. But he understood enough.

"We go to a house at Will's Creek, in the east," he said, to Scarouady. "They will tell us."

"Goodby," uttered Scarouady; and he turned about and made off, and Robert followed close.

So they left Nemacolin the Delaware from the Monongahela to guide Colonel Thomas Cresap, blazing the trail known as Nemacolin's Trail from present Cumberland upon the upper Potomac at Will's Creek in northern Maryland to Redstone Creek of the Monongahela River far in the west.

By this trail the Ohio Company of the Washingtons and others, settling lands between the Alleghany Mountains and the Ohio River, intended to take their goods. By this trail George Washington marched against the French. By this trail General Braddock, with his aide George Washington, marched his army across rivers and over the mountains, to meet the French and Indians in battle near the Forks of the Ohio; and it was named Braddock's Road. And in due time the trail of Nemacolin and the road of Braddock became the National Road of southern Pennsylvania, for travel between the Potomac and the Monongahela, and thence north to Pittsburgh.

So they took the eastward trail, which wended through ravines, through parks, dense forests, around hills, across creeks and over mountains where snow had fallen, until the second evening they were almost in sight of the Potomac of present Maryland.

"I smell smoke," said Scarouady. "Somebody cooks meat." Then they came out into a clearing for a cabin with smoke curling from the mud chimney.

Children ran, a woman screamed, and a man working outside jumped for his gun. But Scarouady shouted "Friend, No 'fraid," and went in, with Robert close at his heels.

"He has a scalp!" the woman cried; and the man still kept his gun ready. Scarouady laughed.

"Mingo, friend of English. Cherokee scalp. Where Washington comp'ny?"

"Washington company?" uttered the man.

"Yep. Washington comp'ny. Will's Creek. Where?"

"He means that Ohio Company that's built a storehouse down near the creek mouth, John, I reckon," spoke the woman.

"Oh! Well, this here creek jines Will's Creek. You foller down to the river an' ask at the big house there, if it's the Ohio Company you're seekin'."

"Goodby," said Scarouady. He and the Hunter trotted away. Robert's moccasins were worn through and his feet were sore, and Scarouady settled into a long wolf stride rather rapid for a boy's tired legs.

"Now we catch Washington soon," said Scarouady over his shoulder.

They could smell the river. It was the Potomac—smelling very different from the creek that they followed. Within a short time they sighted lights, glimmering through the darkness. The forest was dark and cold; the lights were those of a house at the river—and of a camp fire, nearer than the house.

The camp fire, in a sheltered hollow among the black trees, looked inviting. They went down to it. There were horses; and men lying wrapped in blankets, like Indians, their feet to the blaze; and in front of a lean-to of boughs, fronting the fire, two other men, sitting; a young man, in a match coat, or wool blanket-coat, putting marks upon paper, and an older man, well muffled against the night air, smoking a pipe and staring into the fire.

"Washington!" Robert whispered. "You see him!"

Scarouady hailed: "Hallo, English."

One of the men lying down started up; but the old man sitting never moved, and Washington only raised his head, and answered:

"Hallo. Come in, friends."

Scarouady and Robert stepped forward into the fire circle. The old man glanced at them; then he looked at Washington, as if curious to see what Washington would do. He was a large old man, with a tired, thin face, sharp beaked nose, and bulging gray eyes; and he was watching Washington.

Washington sat calmly.

"Our brothers are welcome," he said. The old man nodded as if satisfied. Washington was larger and browner than before, and wore Indian moccasins, leather trousers, and a deer-hide shirt underneath his wool coat, and upon his head a fox-skin cap. This camp at the edge of the thick, frosty forest might have been a thousand miles into the wilderness, for it was a very simple camp—a regular woodsman's camp.

Scarouady was eying Washington; and Scarouady, with his fierce visage, his Oneida paint and his cheeks tattooed with bow-and-arrow, his head shaven except for his scalp lock, and the Cherokee scalp stiff in his belt, might easily have frightened these English.

"It is good," he said. "I seek Washington."

"By George, George!" crackled the old man. "He does? Who's your friend?"

"I am George Washington," said the young chief. "My brother has travelled far. He is an Oneida. Let him sit down and eat and rest." And Washington made the sign for eating and resting.

"George, George!" laughed the old man. "You're gettin' on. Gist could do no better."

The Hunter saw that Washington had learned manners. The first time, he had asked questions; now he asked no questions. Curiosity is impolite. He used the sign language.

He spoke to Scarouady the chief, he read the Oneida paint, he did not appear to recognize Robert who was not a warrior.

Scarouady and Robert sat down, and ate. Washington waited until they were through; then he asked:

"My brother who comes with the Hunter wishes to see me?"

"The Hunter is a boy; be warrior some day. He has more English. He may tell young captain," directed Scarouady. "Speak."

"We come from Tanacharison," Robert explained. "He is Mingo Half-King, on the Ohio. He send Scarouady to say for you to come quick, with company, and build a house with guns to keep the French out."

"George, George!" laughed the old man. "That's what."

"But why does he send to me?" Washington asked.

"Trader says Washington is captain of a company making ready to march and build houses at the Ohio. Tanacharison says for you to come with big guns and he will show you where to build."

"Are the French there now?"

"French been, gone, come again," grunted Scarouady. "Next time come, find big house with guns. Boom!"

"Gad! It's true, then," spoke the old Englishman. "The frontier pot's boilin'; eh, Gist?"

The third man, who was a stout, gray-eyed, red-faced man weathered by sun and wind, heat and cold, nodded.

"Yes, my lord. 'Tis high time for action, or we lose the west and are penned in like sheep."

"French come with soldiers. Bury plates to make the land theirs, and order English out," said Robert. And he insisted: "Washington march his company and stay."

"Tanacharison does not understand," said Washington, gravely. "He has heard of the Ohio Company. That is not my company. I have no company. I am George Washington. It is my brother Lawrence Washington who is head of the company."

"Huh!" said Scarouady. "He chief?"

"A soldier chief. Older than I am."

"Wah!" Scarouady grunted. "Too many Washington. Where he?"

"He is far," replied George Washington, with the sign. "But the company is coming to the Ohio. It is making ready. You tell him, Chris. It's well we've camped here. This man," he added, to Scarouady, "is Christopher Gist, a great trader and hunter."

"Brother," spoke Christopher Gist, in the Mingo dialect, which was a sort of trade tongue used among all the Indians. "I see you are a chief."

"Wah!" said Scarouady.

"You have a Cherokee scalp at your belt. I am from the south." Christopher Gist used signs as well as words. "You are from the north. The Cherokee are wolves that travel between. They are to be struck, so that the road shall be kept open to brothers."

"Wah!" said Scarouady. "It is said. I have heard of my brother. He is called Gist, and the Cherokee fear him. Has he changed his hunting ground?"

"I live upon the river called Yadkin, in the land called North Carolina," said Christopher Gist. "Now I am coming to the Mingo."

"Wah!" exclaimed Scarouady surprised. "Will my brother live among the Mingo?"

"He thinks to do so," said Christopher Gist. "He is coming now to speak with the Mingo for the Washington company?"

"Wah!" Scarouady exclaimed again. "Does Washington come too?"

"Listen, brother," continued Christopher Gist: "You say the French of Onontio are spying out that land and claiming it. We know it is not French land, but Indian land and English land. The Washington Company will march into it and build houses along the Ohio to keep the French out. But first they send me, to learn the trail and to look upon the land and to sit in council with the Mingo so that the Long House of the Iroquois will know the talk."

"Why does not Washington come?" asked Scarouady.

"This Washington does not speak the Indian tongue."

"What does he do here, then?"

"He and that old man have marched with me a little way, to see me start."

"Who is that old man with the hawk nose and glass eyes?"

"He is a great English chief. His English name is Lord Fairfax. He owns all this land to the Shenandoah—the Daughter of the Stars."

"Does he own that house with the lights in it, by the river?" asked Scarouady.

"No. You see the house. That is the great storehouse of the company. It is full of goods for Indian brothers at the Ohio. The company has come this far and only waits for me to mark the trail and open the road to the Ohio."

"Why does not the company send its chief to talk with chiefs?" demanded Scarouady. "Where is the chief Washington?"

"The chief Washington is sick. He cannot travel. But he is this young chief's brother, and he has sent his brother with me to the beginning of the road. His brother that you see is young, but he is wise."

"Well," said Scarouady, "if that is the house of the Washington company and this Washington is here for his brother who is the chief, why does he not sleep in the warm house instead of out here in the cold and dark like a squirrel?"

"Because he does not fear the cold and dark," said Christopher Gist. "His heart is strong. In marking out lands he lives besides the trail and the forest is his house."

Scarouady nodded.

"Wah! That is good. He is a warrior. Do you come, Gist, and open the road to the English and close the road to the French."

"Onondago will permit?" inquired Christopher Gist.

As everybody knew, or should know, the Grand Council of the Six Nations of the Iroquois, at Onondago in New York, would expect to be asked about this matter of white men building houses in the Ohio Country. Scarouady stood up and made a speech.

"For many years, and before I was born," he said, "the Iroquois have been friends of the English. The first French of Onontio helped the Huron dogs against the Iroquois. The hatchets of the Iroquois have not forgotten. The Iroquois have conquered from the big water to the setting sun, they own the country where the Beautiful River flows, and they give the land beyond the mountains to the English. Scarouady and Gist will set out in the morning to open a short road and carry the word that the English are coming with horses and great guns."

Scarouady suddenly held out his hand to George Washington, who took it, and Scarouady tested his grip.

"Wah! I have heard the truth," Scarouady uttered. "Strong hand, strong heart. My young brother is not a squirrel, he is a bear. If his brother is sick, let him himself go upon the road to the Ohio. He has this old hawk for councillor. Now I will sleep."

So he lay down, and likewise did Robert, with their feet to the fire. But the three white men sat up for some time, talking in English.

They talked of the French who threatened to come down from Canada and seize the Ohio Country, beyond the Alleghany Mountains; of the necessity of holding the country for the English King across the water; of the big tracts of lands west of the mountains and along the Ohio, that had been granted by the King to the Ohio Company; of what Christopher Gist should say to the Mingos, the Delawares, the Wyandots, the Shawnees and the Miamis, to win their friendship; and of the chance of war between the English and the French, to see which should keep the country that both claimed.

"You colonists are like a bullock. You have yet to find out your own strength," said the old man.

"That will be found, if France undertakes to drive us. We cannot suffer our traders to be mistreated, sir," said George Washington, "and our trade with the Indians to be cut off."

"Aye," laughed the old man. "You are slow, and stubborn, like English, and admit no attack upon your liberties. I sometimes think that the best part of England has come over here. And out of this war there will arise, I also think, a new race of peoples by a new name."

"And what will that be, my lord?" Christopher Gist inquired.

"Americans, by George."

"How so, sir?" Washington asked.

"You are already Americans in some of your notions," said the old man. "You wish to grow, and you desire to think as you please. That is why you came here. It is your weakness now, for you do not act together. You cannot bring France to terms of yourselves. You will need help from the King, and helped by the King you will learn to use your strength. France certainly will lose. She cannot hold this remote Ohio country, and she will lose her Canada. You colonists will then be free to expand, without a rival shutting you in. An empire lies west of you. You will grow out of your English clothes, and when England tries to remind you that you owe her your humble duty and must pay for her expenses, you will fight."

"Would you think us so ungrateful, sir?" said Washington.

"Ha ha!" the old man chuckled. "One may be thankful for being set up in business, and then object to turning the business over to outside hands. You Americans are born of freedom, and freedom of action by your own vote you will have."

And that proved true; for when these American colonies had grown large and were self-supporting, and England would have taxed their prosperity, without giving them a vote, they did object.

Much of the talk, however, Robert the Hunter, rather sleepy, did not understand. "Americans!" That was something new. Washington was an American. This perhaps explained why he was so different from the traders whom the Indians called English.

He saw that the old man and Christopher Gist talked with George Washington as though he were a man; he had seen that Washington pleased Scarouady; and he felt satisfied and happy. Tanacharison would find that his word about George Washington the American had been true word.

IV
ON THE TRAIL TO THE WEST

Early in the morning they said goodby to George Washington and the old man his friend, and with Christopher Gist took the long back trail for Logstown again.

"Let Gist follow me," Scarouady directed. "Nemacolin's road is one road, but it goes first to his camp and crosses swift waters. We will go straighter by the Warrior Path along Warrior Ridge, and have only one deep water to cross."

They continued by Nemacolin's road a little way; then they left this road into the west for the Monongahela River, and turned north for the Allegheny River above Dekanawida, the Forks of the Ohio where the Monongahela and the Allegheny joined. There they would have the Allegheny to cross with the pack horses, and then they would be on the north or Logstown side of the Ohio.

Christopher Gist had several men and two pack horses. There was snow upon the Great Mountains—the rocky Alleghany Mountains; the footing was bad for horse and man. The forest was getting wintry; cold rains washed the last of the leaves from the trees, and the wolves howled in the night, and the bear and the turkey were fat with acorns.

"Will you speak well of Washington?" the Hunter asked of Scarouady while they travelled.

"He is not the Washington of the company. His brother who is sick is captain of the company," said Scarouady. "This Washington is young, but I can see that he says little, and when he speaks he speaks like a man."

"If his brother is sick, this Washington may be sent to build the big house."

"A treaty must be made with the Onondago council," said Scarouady. "If the French own the lakes they own the waters that flow into the lakes, but the Iroquois and the English own the waters of the Ohio. That has been agreed. The English may build their big houses, with guns, there, and trade, but they may not settle the lands, for the Indians wish to live on the lands."

And neither Scarouady nor Robert knew that the Ohio Company of Virginia and England had been given by the King five hundred thousand acres of lands upon the Ohio, to settle with families. Of this Christopher Gist said nothing. His business now was to examine the lands and bear messages of friendship from Virginia to the Indians.

"What of the Washington I have seen?" Scarouady asked Gist, as still they travelled. "You know him?"

"I know him," Christopher Gist answered. "In years he is a youth, in mind a man. His home is in the woods. For three years he has been traveling about, marking lands. He is the son of a widow."

"Was his father a chief?"

"His father was not a chief, I think; but was a warrior very strong. Now this youth is being taught by that old man Fairfax, who is a great chief and councillor."

"What of his brother who is sick?" asked Scarouady. "He is a chief?"

"He is a soldier captain, but he stays at home. He cannot travel," said Christopher Gist. "There is another brother who stays at home upon his lands, also. This young Washington likewise has lands of his own, but he prefers the woods, that he may learn how to care for himself without help. He is a good hunter and trail finder. I look for him to be a great chief."

"We shall see," replied Scarouady. "He shows much sense."

They marched on, into the north. Gist was sick and had to make stops. And one day Scarouady, leading, leaped back; at the same time Gist's horse shied, almost throwing him. A man stood in the trail. Scarouady cried out:

"The Black Rifle!"

The man was the man that the Hunter remembered; a very large man, black in hair and in beard, and of eye blackly glowing and of skin dark; clad in leather he was like an Indian, with fur cap upon his head. He held his long rifle ready, but lifted his free hand in the talk sign.

"Who are you and what do you want?" he demanded of Gist.

"I am Christopher Gist from the Virginia settlements,

and travel on the King's business," said Gist boldly. "Who are you?"

"Captain Jack of Pennsylvania. The Injuns know me as the 'Black Rifle' or the 'Black Hunter.' How many of the varmints with you?"

"You see two, a chief and a boy," answered Gist. Now other men appeared, among the trees and bushes near—wild, eager men, poising their guns and searching with their eyes. "They guide me and are under my protection. You're an Injun killer, I take it."

"I am," said the Black Rifle. "The Injuns killed mine, I kill them. Where are you going?"

"To talk with the Mingos and the tribes west as far as the Miami, and win them from the French. Do we pass on?"

"Yes," said the Black Rifle, "you may pass on. These are Mingos. My war is with the Delawares and Shawnees; but keep your Injuns close, for all copper skins are apt to look alike over my rifle sights. Are the French seizing the river?"

"So they say."

The Black Rifle laughed harshly as he stepped aside.

"Beware of the Injuns, then. They will talk fair, and then act as they please, for the sake of scalps and plunder. But go ahead; and when you have to fight the French and Injuns both, there will be need of the Black Hunter."

He sprang backward, and was gone; gone were his men, and the forest was silent.

"Wah!" Scarouady exclaimed, breathing hard. "It was he, the killer of the trail. I thank my brother for sending him away."

"The name of your father the King is powerful," answered Gist. "He suffers no harm to come to his children the Indians."

"Well," uttered Scarouady, "let my father the King count his Injuns, then, and ask the Black Rifle what has become of those not found. There can be no peace while the trail is bloody."

The year was late when they all toiled down the hills to old Shanopin's-town beside the Allegheny River just above the Forks.

Here they heard news.

"The trader George Croghan and Sattelihu whom the English call Captain Montour have been here with presents and talk from the Governor of Pennsylvania," said Scarouady. "I know there is jealousy between the men of Onas and the Long Knives of Assaragoa who rules Virginia. We will go ahead of Gist to Logstown and prepare the way."

So they left Christopher Gist to talk with the Delawares of King Shanopin, and then to swim his horses through the swift, cold Allegheny; and they went on to Logstown.

Tanacharison was not here. He was still out hunting. Only White Thunder was here, and a few old men. The trader Croghan and Captain Montour whose Seneca name was Sattelihu had stopped, and gone into the west, bearing presents and peace belts from Pennsylvania to the Miamis of Ohio.

"You have been away a long time, Hunter," Bright Lightning greeted Robert.

"I have been to the Americans," said Robert.

"Who are they?"

"They are the people of the captain Washington, in the Long Knives' country."

"Wah!" Bright Lightning exclaimed. "What do they look like?"

"Like the English. They are white, too; but they differ like the Mohican differs from the Delaware."

"Do the Washington Americans come to build a big house?"

"Not yet," said Robert. "A man named Gist is come to open the trail and look upon the land for the Americans."

"The men of Onas say that the Long Knives of Virginia are coming to settle upon the lands," Bright Lightning informed. "We shall be driven off. The hearts of the people in Logstown are turning bad."

And that was so. When Christopher Gist drove his pack horses down the valley to Logstown he was met with black looks and mutterings.

"You will never get home safe," said Delawares and Shawnees, and even some of the Mingos. "You are here to spy upon the land, and steal it with settlers."

The Pennsylvania traders stationed here laughed, and

encouraged the talk. But Gist acted boldly.

"I am come with a message from the great King across the water," he answered. "He has sent me to his children. I visit all the Indians to bid them to a great council with their other father, the Governor of Virginia, at Logstown this next spring."

"I think you had better go on," Scarouady said to Gist. "Your words shall be spoken by me to Tanacharison, but the forest is better for you than Logstown."

"I think so, myself," replied Gist. "I will catch up with Croghan."

"The Miami have sent a peace belt to the Governor of Pennsylvania, and have told him that their friendship for the English will last while the sun and moon run round the world," stated Scarouady. "Croghan and his men are safe. You should be safe, for you bear peace words from the King our father and from the Governor of Virginia. But to make you safe I will send with you this boy, whose name is the Hunter. Tanacharison is his father. When the Wyandot and the Shawnee and the Miami see that Tanacharison has lent his son to you they will not dare to harm you. Besides, the boy was born in that country. He knows the trails and maybe he will see his mother again on White Woman's Creek. A warrior should not forget his mother."

To protect Christopher Gist and to show him the way, Robert the Hunter rode beside him southward down the wintry Ohio Valley. Soon they cut west across the country for the town of the Wyandots or Little Mingos, on the upper Muskingum River which means Elk's Eye.

Here they caught George Croghan and Captain Andrew Montour, who had been giving out presents. The Wyandots were many. They numbered one hundred families, so that Muskingum of eastern Ohio was larger than Logstown.

The English traders were gathering here. The French Ottawas to the north had captured three traders and sent them to Canada. Part of the Wyandots had been in favor of the French of Onontio, but now George Croghan laughed gaily when he shook hands with Christopher Gist.

"Unpack," he said. "We are brothers. I have raised the flag over my house and over the house of the chief. The

Wyandots say that the French have spread evil in the land with their lead plates and are trying to drive out the traders. We are to hold a council soon. After that we will travel together."

The Wyandots crowded forward to shake hands also with Gist.

"The French of Onontio have broken the chain of friendship," they said. "Let the English come and live with us. Bring great guns and make a fort."

When the council was held Christopher Gist and George Croghan and Captain Montour dressed in their best. Captain Montour was as famous as Captain Joncaire, but was better looking. His mother was half French and half Indian, his father was a Seneca; and he stood high in the councils of the Iroquois. He spoke well in the Iroquois tongues, and was white of skin.

At the council he wore a long coat of reddish cloth, a red vest of satin, a white shirt outside his trousers, which were tucked into his shoes and stockings; around his neck a black tie with silver stars, upon his head a tall, hard hat, in his ears brass wire rings plaited like a basket handle; and his face was painted with a broad circle of bear's grease and blue clay.

He spoke the words of George Croghan, and the Hunter spoke the words of Christopher Gist; and the Wyandots listened.

"We accept the wampum of our brothers from the English of Pennsylvania and of Virginia," they said. "The French have soiled the peace path."

"Your father of Virginia asks you to visit him and receive presents sent by your great father across the water."

"That," the Wyandots answered, "cannot be decided until after the big council at Logstown in the spring."

"We will go on to the Shawnee," said George Croghan.

That pleased Robert. The trail to the Shawnees led across White Woman's Creek, where his mother lived among the Delawares. He found her there, and well.

"What are you doing, travelling with white people?" she asked.

"I am the mouth and ears of Captain Gist who brings peace belts from the Governor of Virginia," he said proudly.

"He is a good man."

"I do not know him, but I know this Croghan," she answered. "He is filling the country with his traders who feed the Indians rum against the law. I remember when I was a girl not as old as you I lived among the white people and they were good. They prayed much and did right. I have seen that as soon as they get into the woods they turn about and cheat and lie and do wrong. I would rather have you stay with Tanacharison, or else come home."

"But all the English are not bad," said Robert. And he had much to tell her, of Washington the American, and the old man, and Christopher Gist. But she would not believe, for through forty years she had seen only the rough traders.

The principal town of the terrible Shawnees, who were light of skin, red of heart, and looked upon the Delawares as grand-fathers, lay in the southwest, at the mouth of the river Sciota in southern Ohio. The Shawnees, like the Delawares, hated the Iroquois who had driven them and the Delawares out of their Pennsylvania homes.

The Shawnees, too, had heard that the French were taking the English traders away from the Indians of the Ohio. They held council with Captain Croghan and Christopher Gist in the great council house ninety feet long and roofed with bark, on the north side of the Ohio, here at Sonnioto.

"The French came, claiming the land," they said. "We shot bullets through their flag. We threatened Captain Joncaire with fire. We would not give up the English traders to them, for the English traders furnish us with plenty of powder. Were it not for the English we would be poor. You may stay among us, and in the spring we will go with you to the big council at Logstown."

But the Miamis were yet to be visited. Their principal town was two hundred miles northward; and they had sent friendship belts to Onas the Governor of Pennsylvania.

The Shawnees pointed out the way, and George Croghan led into the unknown.

The season was early spring. The country was fresh and beautiful, rich with deer and buffalo and turkeys, and grass and noble trees.

After a time they came to the upper Miami River, and

they saw upon the west side the great town Pickawillanee of the Miami nation, where today is Piqua, Ohio.

So they made a raft of logs and branches, and loaded it with the presents and the saddles, and drove their horses into the river. The white men and Captain Montour crossed on the raft, but Robert the Hunter swam with the horses, to keep them going.

The Miamis came out with the peace pipe to meet George Croghan and Christopher Gist. Then under the flag of the English they entered the town, while the warriors fired salutes.

The flag was hoisted over the chief's house. A powerful people, were these Twightwees or Miamis, forming a league as strong as the league of the Iroquois, and ruling all this country clear to the Mississippi. They were haughty, but polite, and swift of foot.

Pickawillanee contained four hundred houses, and many English traders, who had built a fort against the French. The chief was Old Britain of the Piankashaw tribe. The French of Captain Céleron had been here; and as answer to his threats Old Britain had asked the traders to build that fort.

This very afternoon a council was held in the Long House with the messengers from Pennsylvania and Virginia. Captain Montour said, for Croghan and Gist:

"Brothers the Twightwees, we give you two strings of wampum to remove the trouble from your hearts and to clear your eyes to the sunshine. Your brothers the Wyandot and Delaware and Shawnee in the south send you these four strings of wampum and ask you to take care of us."

"Yo ho!" the Miamis grunted, in approval.

"Your brother the Governor of Pennsylvania has heard you speak to him, and he sees that his traders are safe among you," said Captain Montour. "We come with news of great importance, and we hope that you have among you somebody who knows the Mingo tongue, so that we are being understood."

"Yo ho!" the Miamis grunted.

"You see this man Gist, from the Long Knives of the country of Virginia," said Captain Montour. "Tanacharison who is Half-King of the Mingo upon the Ohio, your brothers to the east, out of love has given his son to him, to travel with him and sit beside him. This man also has news for you from your brother the Governor of Virginia."

"Yo ho!" the Miamis grunted.

But not all the Miami tribes were here. The principal men of the Weas and the Piankashaws who lived farther west in Indiana and Illinois had to be sent for.

So another council was set. Gist and Croghan dealt out paint and colored shirts, that the chiefs and councillors might dress for the great event. Robert the Hunter, from Logstown of the Mingo, roaming about Pickawillanee with its bark houses and swarm of Miamis, never before had seen so many Indians together.

At the grand council in the Miami Long House Captain Montour wore his tall hat and his reddish coat and his spangled neckerchief. Sitting in a circle the chiefs and old men and the messengers from the English each took one puff of the great calumet or peace pipe. Then there were speeches. Then the Miami delegates, two from each tribe, signed a treaty with the Governor of Pennsylvania. Old Britain promised Christopher Gist that the Miami should come to the Logstown council and get their presents from the Governor of Virginia.

Then a herald hurried in to say that peace messengers from the French of Onontio were waiting outside.

The Miami shouted in anger; but King Britain stood up beside the English flag and called:

"Silence! This is no way in which to receive messengers. Let those men be admitted and we will hear what they have to say. Then we shall know what to answer."

The messengers came in. They were four Ottawas from the north. The head Ottawa strode proudly through, with the French flag.

"Brothers the Miami," he said, "we are come with the flag of Onontio and with words to strengthen the chain of friendship between the Miami and their French brothers. Onontio wishes to speak through our lips."

"The messenger from Onontio may speak," answered King Britain; so he took the flag and planted it beside the English flag.

"Your father, the French King," the Ottawa said, "remembers his children in the Ohio country, and sends them two kegs of milk and this tobacco for their pipes." The other Ottawas laid down two kegs of brandy and the roll of tobacco. "Your father has, by these, made a clean road for you to come and see him and his officers," the head Ottawa went on; "and he urges you to come, assuring you that all past differences will be forgotten."

But King Britain replied sternly:

"It is true that your French father has sent for us several times, and has said the road to him is clear. But the road is not clear; it is foul and bloody and the French have made it so. We have cleared a road for our brothers the English; now your fathers have made it bad and have taken some of our brothers prisoners. This we look upon as done to ourselves."

With that, King Britain turned his back upon the Ottawas and strode out of the Long House.

The Ottawas pretended to weep.

"We see our brothers the Miami dead," they howled. "The French of our father are like the leaves of the forest, but who are the English? When your father learns of your reply, he will send soldiers with whips to drive you from his land. Woe, woe! All the land will be red, and there will be only widows and small children. The name Miami will be known no more. We weep for the Miami."

The Miamis did not mind; and George Croghan and Christopher Gist laughed. The chief orator of the Miami stood up. He said, to the English:

"You have taken us by the hand into the great chain of friendship. Therefore we give you this bundle of skins, to make shoes for your people, and this pipe to smoke in, to let you know that our hearts are good toward you, our brothers. As for these foolish messengers, they may go back where they came from."

War Chief Whooping Crane stood up:

"French fathers," he called, looking north as if he were speaking to Canada, "you have wished us to go home to you, but I tell you it is not our home. We have made a path to the sun-rising, and have been taken by the hand by our brothers the English, and in that road we shall go. As you threaten us with war in the spring, we tell you, if you are angry we are ready for you, and we will die here before we will go to you. That you may know this is our mind we send you this string of black wampum."

Then he said to the Ottawas:

"Brothers, the Ottawas, you hear what I say. Tell that to your fathers the French, for it is our mind, and we speak it from our hearts."

While the Miamis hooted and defied, the Ottawas were given back their flag and their kegs of "milk" and their tobacco; and still weeping and howling they started off for the French at the Great Lakes. That seemed to settle the French.

The next day there was a grand Feather Dance, most remarkable. Three chief dancers, painted all over, pretended to be birds and jumped about inside a circle, to the beats of a drum, and waved feathered sticks. Warriors struck the post with their hatchets and sang of their great deeds, and threw gifts. The dance lasted half a day.

Then Christopher Gist and the Hunter left George Croghan and Andrew Montour, and the Miamis of Pickawillanee, and started home.

"Tell the Governor of Virginia that our friendship for the English shall stand like the loftiest mountain. We give no heed to the French," Old Britain bade.

So having crossed the river again with Gist, Robert the Hunter rode south, through the rich prairies of Ohio, the two hundred miles to Shawnee town.

"You will have good word for the Washington company," he said. Everything seemed to have turned out well.

"Yes," said Gist.

"Now the French will see they cannot come in, and the Washington company will build their big houses."

"Yes," said Gist. "But the French are quick. They can travel down the rivers again while the men of Virginia are breaking through the mountains."

"Long Knife Americans must get there first and block the road," said the Hunter.

"Americans? Where did you learn that word?" asked

Gist.

"I heard. Washington is American; you are American. Mebbe many Americans in Virginia and Pennsylvania. Not the same as English of the King across the water. Mebbe if you act quick you beat the French."

"Your ears are big. You should be called the Rabbit," laughed Christopher Gist. "Methinks the French are quick and brave, like the eagle; the English are slower, but also brave, and hard to turn when once they have started, like the buffalo. If we Americans, such as you call Washington, are free to act, we may partake of the qualities of both the French and English; but now we are children of the King. Well, from this Shawnee town I go down river to see more country. You will go up river, and tell Tanacharison what we have done. You have been a good boy; the horse you ride is yours."

Then Gist travelled for the south, and Robert turned around and rode home alone, to report to Tanacharison and Scarouady.

He had left Logstown in the last week of November; he arrived at the beginning of the last week of March, having been gone four months.

V

The Young Chief Arrives

The French were coming! The great council of Mingos, Shawnees, Delawares, Wyandots and Miamis had been held at Logstown. Christopher Gist was there and a man named Captain Joseph Fry to sign for Virginia. Washington had stayed home. Gist said that Washington's brother, the sick chief, had died, and Washington was needed to comfort the widow.

The Iroquois from Onondago the council seat did not come.

"We do not meet to talk of business in the woods and weeds," they sent word. "But the English have our permission to use land southeast of the Ohio. We do not give title to that land. The lands of Virginia stop on the sunrise side of the Alleghany Mountains."

So a treaty of friendship was signed with Virginia. Tanacharison himself said, to Gist and Fry:

"Be quick to build us a big fort at the Forks of the Ohio, that will keep the French back. If the chief Washington is dead, let the young Washington bring in the men and build the fort."

But the French were coming. The council had been ended a little time when runners from the west arrived with bad news. Two hundred and fifty Ottawas and Ojibwas of the French, led by Charles Langlade the bold French ranger, had attacked Pickawillanee of the Miamis, and taken it and its English traders, and the Ottawas had eaten old Chief Britain of the Piankashaws!

"Now we see that the French of Onontio are strong," said the King Shingis of the Delawares. "They have conquered the Miami, but the English have done nothing. We had better wait and see."

For the French were coming. Christopher Gist was laying out a town fifty miles southeast of the Forks, near a place called Great Meadows; but the Ohio company were still sitting in their storehouse at Will's Creek on the Potomac, one hundred and fifty miles by trail from the Forks of the Ohio.

And the French were coming. Runners from Onondago arrived. Mohawks had seen a great fleet of French canoes loaded with soldiers making south upon the Great Lakes, to enter the Ohio Country.

The water was covered with boats, said the runners, and the boats bore six thousand soldiers and Indians, to drive the English out of the Ohio country.

Next, the French had landed and had built a fort on the southeastern shore of Lake Erie, from which they could march by land and river to the head of the Allegheny River. And from this place they cut a road through the woods to the River of Buffalo, which emptied into the Allegheny. Here they built another fort; and they would paddle down Buffalo River into the Allegheny, and down the Allegheny to the Forks of the Ohio. They sent men forward under Captain Joncaire to the Seneca and Delaware town of Venango at the mouth of the Buffalo River, and drove Trader John Fraser from his house and took it. Fraser had run away, to live in another house at the Monongahela, south of the Forks.

Now Venango was French; the French were as close as the head of the Allegheny, sixty miles from Logstown, and the American-English of Virginia and of Pennsylvania had not paid any attention, except with words, to the Mingo wampum belts summoning aid.

"The French will build a line of forts all down the Ohio, and shut us from the English traders," said Tanacharison. "Where is that Ohio Company, who have permission to build a fort for us? If we go to war with the French we lose our lands."

And many of the Delawares and Mingos and Shawnees began to think that the English of Virginia and Pennsylvania were weak.

At last a man came, sent by the Governor of Virginia, to warn the French to stay back out of the country. His name was Captain William Trent. From Logstown he marched northwest, to find the French commander. But in a little time he was back again. When he had reached Pickawillanee he found only the French flag flying over the burned fort and houses, and his heart turned over. He did nothing at all.

"That man is a coward," said Tanacharison. "He is afraid of the French, but I am not. I will go, myself, to the French at Lake Erie and find the head soldier, and tell him what he must do."

Tanacharison was gone a month. Then he, too, came back. He had talked with the French chief, and had tried to return the peace belt which held the Mingos to the French. The French chief had laughed at him, and called him "child"—had thrown the belt in his face and ordered him home.

A Delaware who had been at Venango brought word to Logstown that the French were coming down in the spring; if the Indians meddled the Indians would be killed while the English were being conquered; and even if the English kept part of the lands, the other lands would go to the French and the Indians would have nothing. This was the warning sent by Captain Joncaire.

"If the English do not help us this fall, in the spring they will be too late," said Tanacharison. "For in the spring when the waters are high the French will bring their canoes and men while the English are kept back by the snows in the mountains. Why do the men of Virginia sit with their hands between their knees?"

The Half-King sent a string of wampum to Trader Fraser's house in the south on the Monongahela, and a speech for Assaragoa the Governor of Virginia, telling him that the Chippewas, the Ottawas and the Adirondacks of the north had taken up the hatchet for the French; he should hurry many men. Then, having done all that he could, the Half-King went hunting.

Scarouady stayed. If word came from the Governor, Robert was to carry it to Tanacharison at his hunting cabin.

Then, when Tanacharison had been gone only a few days, great news broke.

It was Robert who made the discovery. Early in the morning he had ridden up the Ohio, to hunt on the other side of the Meeting of the Waters. He kept a little canoe hidden in the bushes at the Forks, just for that purpose.

He passed King Shingis's town, across the Ohio; and leaving his horse he was going for his canoe, when he saw two men among the trees of the bank opposite.

They were on horses, and so they were English; Indians travelled afoot. And he could see that they were white men, anyway. Thereupon the Hunter shoved right out and paddled over, and found George Washington waiting for him.

"Hallo!" Washington greeted. "It is the Hunter again. Welcome, Hunter."

"Welcome, Washington," Robert answered. "You build fort?"

The other man he did not know. That was a stout man, with a face like a wrinkled persimmon, and with red nose, very blue eyes, and the yellow hair of his chin cut to a point like a tuft of a lynx ear. He wore a uniform of old blue coat, buttoned tight, and pants tucked into boots.

Washington wore a three cornered hat, and a blue coat with white facings and bright buttons and tails turned back, tight breeches and boots. It looked like a soldier chief's dress.

"This is a good place for a fort," said Washington. "But I do not build it. I am going on."

"You come Logstown with company?" asked the Hunter.

"Yes, to Logstown. Is the Half-King there?"

"Half-King gone hunting. He leave Scarouady and me to wait if any word come from English. You bring Long Knife Americans, Washington?"

"My men follow with a canoe so that we can cross," said Washington.

"It iss a goot friend of yours, major?" spoke the stout, red-nosed man, in English hard to understand.

"He is the boy who showed me how to wade a stream by carrying a rock," answered Washington. "Half-King is his father."

Washington remembered. That had been several years ago; he seemed much older now, and the Hunter had grown, too. But he remembered.

Other men came. They were Christopher Gist and John Davidson the trader. They had left a third man to wait for the men bringing a canoe down from John Fraser's place up the Monongahela.

Washington talked with Gist and Davidson. He had been looking at the land here in the Forks and had seen what

Tanacharison had seen long ago—that it was the best place for a house with big guns.

"It lies high and level," said Washington, "and commands the two rivers and the entrance to the Ohio. By the Monongahela we could travel to and from the Virginia outposts in the south, and no one from the north could pass out of the Allegheny."

"Yah, it iss the proper meelitary situation," said the red-nosed man. "Dere iss no better."

"The spot where I was told to start a fort for the Ohio Company is yonder across the Monongahela, and two miles down the Ohio," said Gist. "That's where old Shingis of the Delawares lives, on the south bank. Do you wish to stop and see him, major?"

"Yes, we'll stop and invite him to our council at Logstown," replied Washington.

"How stands Shingis now? Is he friendly to the English?" asked John Davidson, in the Mingo, of Robert.

"The Delawares are of two minds," answered Robert. "They wait. If the English are strong and give presents, Shingis will be English. If the French are strong and give presents, Shingis will be French. Let Washington talk with him. Who is that fat man with the red nose and the tight shirt? Is he American?"

"Ho ho!" laughed Davidson. "What is that word—American? You see Americans, but you see English, too. That man's name is Jacob Vanbraam. He is a soldier captain from another white man's country across the big water which they call Dutch Land. But now he is American-English. He teaches Washington to use the big knife which in English is sword; he speaks the French language and he goes with Washington to talk to the French in the north. We ask Tanacharison to help us on the trail."

"Wah!" exclaimed the Hunter. "Is Washington a chief?"

"He is a major in the army of Virginia, and commands soldiers."

"Wah!" uttered Robert. "That is good. He is a man. Tell him I will be a warrior under him, to fight the French. Now I go and tell Scarouady Washington is come against the French, and to make ready."

Then the Hunter ran for his canoe. When he shoved out, the canoe from John Fraser's, with two men in it, was coming in to meet Washington. The Hunter paddled across, and got on his horse and went at a gallop, full of news for Logstown.

First he saw Bright Lightning.

"What is it? The French?" she asked.

"It is Washington with men, for Logstown."

"Many?"

"I saw six."

"What can six do?" said Bright Lightning. "You are in a great hurry about one man and five! The French have a thousand. Your Long Knives are fools."

The hunter next met old Juskakaka or Green Grasshopper, the principal councillor; and almost ran into him.

"What is this?" growled Juskakaka. "You are half white and have no manners."

"Washington is come."

"Where is he?"

"At Dekanawida. I saw him."

"With men?"

"Five men."

"Wah!" scoffed old Little Billy. "Does the Governor of Virginia sent a boy and five men to fight the French? It is true what the French say, that the English are blind and have no regard for the Indians."

Next Robert found Scarouady, lying in his lodge.

"What do you want, entering a chief's lodge this way?"

"The Americans are come. I have seen Washington."

"How many?"

"Six, with Washington."

"Where?"

"They are crossing the Forks, to visit King Shingis."

"King Shingis? Don't they know their way to the Mingo, where the head chief of all lives?"

"They come here, too."

"What Washington?"

"The young Washington; the same we saw."

"Wah!" grunted Scarouady. "What does he want?"

"He will talk with Tanacharison and then he goes to the

French."

"The Governor of Virginia sent one man to the French, and he grew afraid and ran home," said Scarouady. "Now Assaragoa sends a boy. The French will laugh. The Mingo do not wish boys with speech belts; they wish men with big guns, to build a fort. But I will see this Washington again, and if it is worth while for Tanacharison to see him, we will send for Tanacharison."

And—

"A boy with five men is very little," agreed White Thunder. "Where is the company, to build the house we asked them to build?"

Washington and the others came at sunset, down the valley; and King Shingis was with them. The men set up a tent, while everybody watched curiously; but John Davidson inquired where Scarouady was, and he and Washington went to the lodge.

"Is that your Washington?" Bright Lightning asked of the Hunter.

"Yes."

"Is he a chief?"

"He is a soldier major of the Long Knife army. The French send us only captains."

"Well," said Bright Lightning, "Old Juskakaka calls him a boy, but I can see that he is a man. The Governor of Virginia has not acted so foolishly after all."

Scarouady and White Thunder and Juskakaka came to Washington's tent, for presents of food. On the way Scarouady called to Robert.

"It is dark now, but in the morning you will go and bring Tanacharison. Tell him Major George Washington has come from Virginia to speak with the French, and wishes to hold council with the chiefs of the Ohio."

Something in Scarouady's tone told the Hunter that George Washington had proved to be strong.

VI

BY ORDER OF THE GOVERNOR

Tanacharison's hunting cabin was on Little Beaver Creek, fifteen miles down the Ohio. When the Hunter found him in the morning, he was in no hurry to meet Washington.

"Instead of sending us a principal man," he said, "the Governor of Virginia sends a boy without experience to talk with chiefs. I am Half-King and wish to talk with Assaragoa himself. He rules Virginia, and I rule my country. It is not dignified for me to run at the call of a boy. But I will go up during the day, when I have finished my business here."

So it was not until the middle of the afternoon that Tanacharison arrived in Logstown. He went to his own house, to change his clothes. But George Washington acted sensibly. Pretty soon he came to the house with John Davidson, who spoke Iroquois dialects, and after greeting Tanacharison he said:

"I am arrived at Logstown from your brother the Governor of Virginia, to talk with the Mingo, the Delaware, the Shawnee, the Wyandot. If Tanacharison, who is Half-King, will come to my tent, we can speak there in private away from the ears of women and children."

Tanacharison looked Washington up and down.

"That is well said," he answered. "You are young, but you have wisdom. This boy may come, to be present in case I do not understand. You know him. He is my son."

Therefore the Hunter went with Tanacharison and Washington to Washington's tent, and they sat down.

"I am told," said Washington, "that you went, yourself, to the French chief at the Lakes, and commanded him to leave. As I am going there too, I should like to know what your words were to him and what his words were to you, and what the distance is, so that I may know how to act."

"When I went, the distance was shorter," replied the Half-King. "You are too late in the year to get there easily. The snows and rains have swollen the rivers and made many great bogs. The first fort is at least six nights' sleeps by best travel."

"Nevertheless, I am going," said Washington. "Those are my orders from the Governor."

"Me the French insulted. You they will laugh at, and think to fool, because you have no beard," objected Tanacharison.

"If they think I am not worthy of notice," Washington said quietly, "then they will not watch me and I can look about and see what they have."

"Wah!" Half-King uttered. "The other man was a coward. You are no coward. I see you will go to the French chief."

"If my brother will tell me what he said to the French chief and what the French chief answered, I will listen," Washington prompted.

"The French chief treated me like a dog," declared Tanacharison, growing angry. "He has since died; now there is another, and what his mind is I do not know. I went alone to see the first, who commanded last summer. I took the speech belt of friendship left us by Captain Joncaire. Instead of being polite and receiving me like a chief, the Frenchman sat down while I stood and he asked me who I was and what was my business there. I said to him:

"'Father, a long time ago you set before the Six Nations a basin with the leg of a beaver, and bade us eat in peace and plenty; and if any person disturbed us, we should drive him out.'

"'Now, father it is you who are disturbing us, by coming and building on our lands, and taking it away.'

"'Father,' I said, 'a long time ago we kindled a fire for you at a place called Montreal, where you were to stay. I now ask you to go to that place, for this is our land and not yours.'

"'Father,' I said, 'if you had come peaceably, like our brothers the English, you could have traded with us like they do. But to come and build houses without our permission and take our land by force we cannot allow.'

"'Father,' I said, 'you and the English are white. We live in a country between; the land does not belong to either of you. Now I ask you to go out. I am saying the same to our brothers the English, and we will see which of you will pay attention and deserve sharing with us. I am here to say this to you, for I am not afraid to order you off our land.' Then I handed the wampum belt to him, that he might know we were done with him."

"Those were good words," Washington nodded gravely. "What did he reply?"

"He said to me, speaking very rudely: 'My child, I do not know this wampum with which you order me away. You need not speak, for I will not hear you. I am not afraid of flies or mosquitoes, such as Indians are. Down the river I will go and build upon it. If the river is blocked I am strong enough to burst it open and tread everybody under my feet.'

"Then he threw the speech belt in my face, and he said, laughing at me:

"'Child, you talk foolish. You say this land belongs to you, but there is not so much as the black of your nail yours. I saw that land before the Six Nations took it from the Shawnees. With lead I went down and took possession of that river. It is my land and I will have it, no matter who tries to stand against me. If you will be ruled by me you will get kindness, but not otherwise.'

"He spoke angrily, with a red face," Tanacharison continued. "So I took the speech belt and came home. You had better think a while before you go, for you will be treated with rudeness."

"My chief the Governor of Virginia has ordered me to travel straight to the French and give the French chief a letter," said Washington. "There I will go!"

"What is in the letter?" Tanacharison asked.

"It is a letter of much importance to us all," said Washington. "And by this string of wampum Assaragoa asks you, his brothers, for young men who will go with me by the shortest road, and hunt for meat, and help me against the French Indians who have taken up the hatchet."

"All this must come before the council tomorrow," answered Tanacharison, "when the chiefs of the Shawnee and the Delaware will be present. But we should like to know your business with the French chief, and what the English intend to do. Do the English claim this land north of the river?"

"The first thing to do is to get rid of the French," said Washington.

"That is so," agreed Tanacharison, growing angry again. "Now I will show you where those French forts are."

Then Tanacharison took a bit of charcoal from the fire, and a strip of bark from a log, and drew pictures.

"The trail to the north is this way," he said. "In so many sleeps," and he six times made the motion of drawing a blanket over his face, "we come to this place named Venango. It stands where the River of the Buffalo empties into the River Allegheny. The French under Captain Joncaire have seized it. And by six more sleeps, up at the other end of the River of the Buffalo, is the second French fort, where the head captain lives. There is a third fort farther on, at the Lake Erie, but you will not need to go to it, I think."

The council with Washington was held the next morning, and much was said. But this did not finish matters. The Mingo speech belt from the French was down at Tanacharison's hunting cabin. The Shawnees had a speech belt and so had the Delawares, and these were to be thrown at the French. Besides, the Shawnee chiefs from Sonnioto down the river had not yet come for council; they would not arrive until after two days.

"This cannot be done in a hurry," the Half-King said to Washington. "I have sent to the Shawnees, for their belt and two young men to go with you. I have ordered Shingis to his town, to bring the Delaware belt and two young men to go with you. When the French see that you have Mingo, Shawnee and Delaware with you, they will know who are your friends."

But King Shingis did not come back. He pretended that his wife was sick, and that all his young men were out hunting. The Delaware speech belt, he said, was up at Venango, with the Delawares there; and he sent a string of wampum which would order the Venango Delaware chief to take the belt on to the principal French fort.

Scarouady declared that old Shingis was afraid. The Delawares all were suspicious yet. The Shawnees stayed away. The Wyandots said:

"Where are the presents the Ohio Company should send

us, if we are to help fight the French? If the French are driven off who will protect us from the English?"

And the Mingos said:

"We do not know what this Washington wishes with the French. What will the English of Virginia do? They can build a trading house with guns, but we will not have our lands stolen from us."

Washington had been in Logstown seven days. Then Tanacharison decided not to wait any longer for the Shawnees and the Delawares. This night he said to Washington:

"We will start for the French fort in the morning, two hours after sunrise. I will go, and we will take Juskakaka to speak for us, and White Thunder who is Keeper of the Wampum; and of all my young men I can find only Guyasuta. But he is active and a brave warrior. Scarouady will stay here to command in my absence."

Then Washington said, through John Davidson:

"I hear your boy is rightly named the Hunter. He looks like a strong boy, and I see he is a smart boy. It is well that he learn what he can, in the company of chiefs. Let us take him to find the game."

"Wah!" uttered Tanacharison, as if pleased. "Yes, he is a fine hunter. There is no better. He also knows the English tongue and the French tongue, and may be useful. We will take him."

When Robert heard this from Christopher Gist, he, too, was pleased. He felt warmly toward George Washington the American.

VII
ROBERT PROVES HIS VALOR

So they all set out, this morning of the day that the English called the last day of November. There were Washington, Christopher Gist, John Davidson the trader who spoke Mingo, the funny, fat Jacob Vanbraam of Dutch Land who spoke French and poor English, Tanacharison the Half-King of the Mingos, old Juskakaka the councillor, White Thunder the Wampum Keeper, young Guyasuta or Standing Cross the first-class warrior, Robert the Hunter and four white men to drive the pack-horses and make camps.

The white men all rode, but the Indians marched afoot, and Robert left his horse at Logstown. In the woods one could hunt more easily afoot than ahorse.

That was indeed a tough journey. Venango, Tanacharison said, was sixty miles by summer trail but was farther now, by winter trail. Already the trees and meadows were white, and the nights were freezing cold. The weather seemed to get angry again, as if trying to close the road for Washington; it had been angry ever since he had started, he said.

On the day after the first camp out from Logstown the sleety rain began to fall, and clear to Venango they scarcely glimpsed the sun or the stars. The creeks were swollen, the trail was slippery, dry wood for burning was hard to find.

But Washington made no complaint. At night in his tent by the light of his smoky fire he put marks upon paper in a little book that he carried. After talking a while and listening to stories in Mingo and sign language by Tanacharison and old Juskakaka and White Thunder, he and Gist and Jacob Vanbraam rolled in their blankets inside the tent. The others slept outside under brush lean-tos covered with blankets.

"The Hunter is young. He may sleep in the tent and be warm between us," Washington had invited. But Tanacharison answered:

"No. The boy is of warrior age. He shall sleep like an Indian, for he cannot carry a tent with him on the war trail. It is proper that you, the white chief, shall keep your message safe in your lodge. We know that you are strong."

"If we meet with the French Indians, do we fight?" Guyasuta had asked.

"It seems to me a poor plan to lose scalps for these English when we don't know what is going to happen," said old Juskakaka.

"Those are small words," Tanacharison reproved. "Washington is not a man to turn back. I see that. We have come to protect him and to show him the road. The French dogs must get out of the way. The war belt has been passed from the Mingo to Onondago of the Six Nations Council, and if the French refuse to quit the land, there is war. Pickawillanee of our brothers the Miami has been destroyed by the French. Already the Miami have taken Ottawa scalps, and the Wyandot have eaten ten white French and two French black men. If Washington fights we will fight, and show him we are standing with him and the English."

Those were lean marches. The rain spoiled the food in the packs and drove the game to cover. It wet the guns and loosened Robert's sinew bow-string; and two deer were all that he and Guyasuta were able to get. What were two deer among twelve men and an empty boy?

So the third evening's camp was a hungry one. The rain had changed to snow, and leaving early after the halt Guyasuta went one way and the Hunter another, to find meat.

The Hunter prowled some little distance, through the snowy forest, seeking fresh tracks or a moving animal. The snow had covered all the old tracks and trails, the great forest seemed lifeless. Now if he only could find a turkeys' roost—! But he saw no turkeys in the bare trees, and he saw no glint of deer, and he heard no sound except a squawking jay who told the forest that a hunter was abroad. Even the squirrels were in bed.

Then after a time he came to a large tree, with its inside hollowed out, for it had a hole wide enough for a boy, at its base. Whether anything had gone into that hole he could not tell, because of the snow, but sometimes wild animals lived in such places.

At any rate, nothing had gone in recently; the new snow was unmarked. Then he stooped, to try to see up into the hollow; he could not see far, for the hollow was dark and extended a long way; but he *smelt*—and the hollow smelled of warm fur.

Wah! The Hunter sprang backward, and eyed the tree. The tree was breathing! From a knothole high up where a branch had once joined the trunk a thin waft of vapor like steam was floating out into the cold air. This tree was inhabited. That vapor came from live animals.

Wah! And again—Wah! Raccoons! Likely enough a family of raccoons; and fat coons were not to be despised by hungry people. Whereupon the Hunter went to work. He raked together the few dry leaves and the damp leaves, in the hollow, and with flint and steel he started his smudge. The draught took the smoke inside and up through the shell of the trunk and it poured out of the knothole. He stood ready with a branch for a club; there was no use in fooling with bow and arrow.

He did not have long to wait. First he heard a scratching, as though the inhabitants of the tree were growing uncomfortable. And on a sudden, with a plump, down dropped a big bunch of fur and rolled out; and instead of springing with his club the Hunter jumped back, to grab his bow and fit arrow to string. For the animal was a bear.

The bear, half-grown and fat, sat up whimpering crossly at having been disturbed; and rubbed its eyes and muzzle with its clumsy paws. The mark was a splendid mark; Robert drew arrow to its head—and did not let go. Instead, he lowered his bow, and laughed.

"I will not kill you, brother," he said. "I am hungry, but I give you your life because your mother saved me from the Cherokee. Do not blame me for putting smoke into your eyes. You shall go back and sleep."

The bear was still rubbing his eyes and complaining. The Hunter stole around him and scattered the smoking leaves.

"The way is clear, brother," said the Hunter; and he went a little distance, and looked back, and saw the bear just disappearing into the hollow again.

"Wah!" Robert remarked. "He was fat meat, and we all are hungry, but maybe I will find something else."

Prowling on he stopped next at a cave under a rock ledge,

much like the place in which White Thunder and Aroas and he had slept when upon the march to the Delawares, only deeper.

Dusk was gathering in the forest. Peering into the cave he could see white bones; he also heard a faint rustle; but what made the rustle he could not see, for the cave was crooked. But something growled low, and that was not a bear.

The bones were not bones from a bear feast, either; clean picked they were, but were not crushed. The Hunter cautiously crawled in, stooping, his bow and arrow advanced ready to be drawn and loosed. His nose told him of animals. The rustling had ceased, but the growling announced that the animal was at home. The floor rose, so that the space between floor and roof grew narrower; and when he came to a black hole just about large enough for him, but not large enough to turn around in, he stopped. All the cave was humming with that growl.

"Whoever you are, you are not good eating," said the Hunter. "Stay there, for I am going."

Maybe the animal answered "Sour grapes" and maybe it only laughed. Anyway, Robert began to crawl backward; and then his feet twitched, and he felt like hurrying, for he heard another, louder growl behind him. Hurry he did, until he could twist about. And when he straightened up, at the threshold, he confronted the owner of the cave.

Not more than fifteen feet before him there crouched, upon the body of a yearling deer, a mother panther, returned (likewise in a hurry) with meat for her family.

The face of the cliff curved in two horns, so that the Hunter had little choice of directions. The panther squatted more flatly, her tail lashing, her long, sharp claws clutching and rasping upon the snow, her tremendous fangs bared to the red gums, while her growls rose to a scream. In the dusk her eyes shone greenly.

Watching her, the Hunter hesitated. To be sure, he might climb the cliff face, if he moved carefully and threatened her off. Then perhaps she would go inside. But Guyasuta would ask him why he had run away. Besides, here was a deer.

"Leave me that deer and you shall have your life," spoke the Hunter. "I have not harmed your babies. You can get another deer. Wah! Out of the way!"

The panther screamed with cat scream, and quivered tensely. She was about to spring. The Hunter, standing stanchly, put one arrow between his teeth and drew the nocked arrow full to the head. He scarce had time—right into the air she launched herself, and he loosed and dodged, and slipped. Her leap was short; as she landed and struck and bit he glimpsed his arrow in her shoulder, but the claws of her sound forearm ripped through leggins and flesh to the bone.

He jumped aside, not to run but to shoot again. He was very quick, and she was quick too. This was a battle to the death. Snarling and tumbling and biting at the arrow she whirled for him; and poised firmly, waiting his chance, he loosed the second arrow just as she rose.

The bow twanged of itself, as it seemed to him; the arrow thudded; she barely had left the ground when she collapsed, for the arrow was buried to the feathers in her chest. She struggled but an instant, and surrendered.

The Hunter gave a scalp yell—"Wah hoo-oo-oo!" Not often did a boy with bow and arrow kill a panther in hand-to-hand battle. What a great beast this was—as large as himself! What teeth, what jaws, what claws! Now he was entitled to wear the panther claw necklace, token of a hunter and a warrior! And he had the deer.

He set to work at once, with his knife, skinning his enemy; and he cut and slashed rapidly for dusk was thickening, and the evening was cold. Very soon he had the pelt. His leg hurt furiously, but that should be looked at later. Then he dressed the deer carcass by removing its insides to make it lighter.

"Listen, brothers," he called, into the cave mouth. "I am leaving you the meat of your mother and the insides of the deer. They will make you strong to hunt for yourselves."

Then he set off, dragging the deer and carrying the panther pelt. The young panthers were large enough to eat meat; they would find rabbits and partridges, and would not starve.

So, well content, and wondering what Washington would say, he staggered along. The raw pelt was heavy, the deer carcass weighed not a little, the forest had waxed gloomy—

and hark! Wolves howled! They were scenting his bloody trail!

Wah! He dared not stop, for his leg would stiffen. He had no mind to lose the pelt, or the deer. Ho! The camp could not be very far, but if he shouted he might attract French Indians in addition to the wolves. One never could tell. He knew a scheme, though. Thereupon he halted and peeled off his hunting shirt; he hung this upon a bit of brush over the deer carcass, to keep the suspicious wolves at a distance; he dragged the panther skin on, for another trail, then he wrapped the skin about his body for warmth, and with the long tail and the feet dangling he limped at best pace to reach the camp. Let the wolves follow.

After a time he smelled smoke. A fearsome sight he was when he hobbled in out of the darkness—a bare-headed brown boy clad from shoulders to ankles in a flapping panther hide, his bow in his hand and his arms smeared and his leg bloody. Wah!

"Wah!" uttered Tanacharison, and all. "The Hunter has taken a scalp! Good!"

"Well done," said Washington. "A large panther. The boy is a hunter. But he is hurt. Sit down and let us look at that leg."

"Where is the meat?" demanded Tanacharison.

"I left a deer in the brush, with my shirt on it to scare off the wolves," panted Robert. "It should be brought quick."

Guyasuta was here. He had returned with nothing. Now he sprang up and ran away, to back-trail to the deer carcass. The Hunter thankfully sat down by the fire; he was proud, but he did not show it—he only told about the fight, while they listened and John Davidson and Jacob Vanbraam, helped by Washington, dressed his wound.

"He iss a brave boy," Jacob Vanbraam declared. "He will make a soldier. Yah! Now pretty soon coom a deer, an' we eat."

George Washington said little, but he nodded and gravely smiled.

VIII

WASHINGTON MEETS THE FRENCH

"The Hunter may ride my horse," proposed Washington, in the morning—and that showed his kind heart.

"No," Tanacharison replied. "It is not seemly. The English chief cannot march afoot in the mud. His feet will wear out. He is too heavy for his horse to bear double; he is a large man. If the boy cannot walk, we will make a litter for him; but I think that with a lift now and then he will suffer no harm. The wounds of the young heal quickly, and he must learn to endure like a warrior."

It took five days to travel the seventy miles. In the afternoon of the fifth day, while they were following a trail up along the black Allegheny River, and the gaunt storm-drenched forest was darkening with early dusk, they came to the edge of the trees and Tanacharison, in the lead, said:

"Venango."

"Gist, do you pitch camp in the cover of the woods," Washington ordered, "whilst I go in with Vanbraam and find the commander. Keep the party together. We will spend the night here." Then he looked at Robert and saw that the leg was swollen and painful; so he added: "The young Hunter with the panther-claw necklace shall come with me. These French may have good medicine for his leg."

"He may go," Tanacharison now responded, pleased. "The leg needs rest by a fire, indoors." And he said to Robert, in Seneca: "You will stay with Washington and learn what is done, so as to tell me."

For Juskakaka and White Thunder, and even Half-King, were still wondering what words Washington was bringing from the Governor of Virginia. Perhaps a bargain was proposed, and the French were to have one side of the Beautiful River and the English the other side, and the Indians would have nothing—just as Captain Joncaire had threatened.

Washington and Vanbraam left their horses and with Robert went afoot into the clearing. They saw before them a great log house, with smoke pouring from the chimney. Separated from it were bark and skin lodges of Delawares, Wyandots and French Indians who lived there. And beyond the house and the lodges was a creek flowing into the Allegheny River, both bordered by the stumps of the clearing.

But the log house was the main thing. Washington said suddenly:

"There's a sight to heat the blood, Vanbraam."

The wind, blowing gustily so that the forest moaned, had whipped a flag, hoisted over the house, into plain sight, flat against the dun sky. It was the flag of France.

"That's likely the trading house Fraser built, and was driven from," continued Washington. "They're bold fellows, those French, to fly their flag in the territory of the King in America, and drive out his American subjects."

This was how it seemed to Robert also, limping on. The French were bold; they travelled far through the woods, and paddled down the rivers and up the rivers, and made merry. Nothing daunted them. And while, of course, he was their enemy, he hoped that they would let him and Washington and Captain Vanbraam in, for his leg was hurting cruelly.

Scarcely any sign of life, except the smoke, appeared in the clearing. But now the Indian dogs began to bark, and evidently they three, maybe all the party, had been seen; for when they were nearing the log house, with Washington ahead, three men stepped out and came a little way to meet them.

The three were French—French officers, by their laced uniform coats, their swords and cocked hats. The first one, lean and active, and dark, Robert knew at a glance.

Then Washington lifted his hat, and Captain Vanbraam stiffly lifted his hat, and the three Frenchmen lifted their hats, so that the chief bared his gray hair.

"I am Major George Washington of his Britannic Majesty's Colony of Virginia," Washington said, for Captain Vanbraam to translate into French. "Will you do me the honor to direct me to the commander of this post."

Bowing and smiling, the gray-haired, wiry man answered, in French that Robert partially understood, because his mother spoke both English and French:

"I have the great pleasure of presenting in myself Captain Chabert de Joncaire, appointed to command for the King of France in the country of the River Ohio."

"Then I have a letter for you, as commander, from the Governor of Virginia, sir," announced Washington. "When I have delivered it at the proper place, I am bidden to wait for an answer."

"Oh, pardon, monsieur," Captain Joncaire smiled. "How is the letter addressed?"

"To the commander of the French forces upon the Ohio, sir."

"Ah," said Captain Joncaire. "It is official. In that case, monsieur, I think it would better be delivered to the Chevalier Legardeur de Saint-Pierre, my superior officer, at Fort le Boeuf."

"And where is that, sir?"

"It is sixty miles to the north, up this Buffalo Creek which we call French Creek, monsieur. A very bad trail. You should not try without resting. You have come a long way to deliver a letter. The letter is important?"

"It is important, sir."

"Tomorrow, then, to Fort Buffalo, if you wish," said Captain Joncaire. "What terrible weather! And now will you and your companion do me the honor to have supper with us. We have little—it is the fare of a soldier, monsieur; but you are a soldier, so why do I apologize?"

"I accept with great pleasure, sir," replied Washington. He introduced Jacob Vanbraam, and Captain Joncaire introduced his two officers, and there was much bowing and saluting and smiling on the part of the three Frenchmen, Captain Joncaire in particular.

Captain Joncaire looked sharply at Robert.

"And who is this?" he inquired.

"An Indian boy whom I have with me," said Washington. "His leg is hurt, as you see, and I am trusting to get it freshly dressed by some of your people."

"He may go to the other Indians in those lodges yonder," said Captain Joncaire. "The Delaware women will dress it."

"Your pardon, sir," objected Washington. "I am responsible for him, and as he is a boy I thought that he might have a corner near me in quarters somewhat warmer than an Indian lodge."

Captain Joncaire shrugged his shoulders and made a little grimace.

"Very well, Monsieur the Major. He may have his corner. But the place for Indians and dogs is out of doors."

That, coming from Captain Joncaire, who was part Indian himself, sounded rather airy.

Now they all proceeded to the large log house. Once the Hunter had thought Captain Joncaire, and Andrew Montour also, to be wonderful persons. But beside Washington, dignified even in his soaked and ragged clothes, and overtopping the three French by a full head, Captain Joncaire and his officers looked small.

A huge fire was blazing hotly in the large main room of the old trading house. There were benches, and a plank table set for supper. A Delaware woman was sent for, and came and dressed Robert's leg. Then at a signal from Captain Joncaire and a nod from Washington he lay down out of the way, upon a bear-skin, near the fire.

Servants began to add dishes and jugs and bottles to the other things upon the table, and brought in roasts of bear, deer and turkeys, a pudding, and heaps of little cakes, and jars of preserves—many things that were strange to Robert, but all looking mighty good.

Candles in brackets were placed upon the table, and the glasses and the dishes shone brightly. Washington and Jacob Vanbraam had removed their heavy coats, and had washed. All sat down at the table. It was to be a feast. Servants passed dishes to them, with meat that had been cut. Never in his life had Robert the Hunter been so hungry. Then Captain Joncaire, with a little cry—"Here, child!"—tossed him a meaty bone to gnaw. But Washington said, politely: "With your permission, monsieur," and got up and coming with his own piled-up plate handed it to the Hunter.

"This is yours, my brave boy," he said. "I know what hunger is, myself."

The Frenchmen stared as if they could scarcely believe their eyes. Captain Joncaire laughed gaily.

"My word, monsieur!" he exclaimed in the French. "You

have the grand manner to an Indian whelp. But you omit. I, Captain, Chabert de Joncaire, will supply. Here, Jacques—" and he filled a tumbler with wine and passed it to a servant: "This for the young seigneur in the corner, that he may drink to His Gracious Majesty the King of France."

Washington stretched out his arm and stopped the servant, and set the glass upon the table again.

"No, monsieur, if you please," he said. He gazed straight at Captain Joncaire. "Water is the sufficient drink, as I have found, myself; and I would not wish to heat his blood."

Again Captain Joncaire laughed. He and the two other French, and Captain Vanbraam, touched water scarcely at all. They drank repeatedly of wine and of brandy, while they ate; but Washington, the Hunter saw, scarcely wet his lips except with water.

After a time the chatter had increased. The meats were removed, but the liquors remained, and the cakes were passed. The three French were red of face, and bright of eye; Jacob Vanbraam was a little flushed, but not much so. Washington sat quietly, letting Vanbraam and the French do most of the talking, and mainly bowing reply to a question or a salute.

He spoke no French; Jacob Vanbraam, however, spoke the French. Every little while he uttered a sentence or two in English, that Washington should know what was being said.

The Hunter was sleepy; but Tanacharison had bidden him keep his ears open, so he only pretended to sleep.

The French were getting drunk and boastful. They talked rapidly, sometimes all together, and Captain Vanbraam made them laugh with his poor French, and they thought him drunk, too, and let him say to Washington whatever he pleased.

"Down we go, in the spring," bragged Captain Joncaire. "Down to the Beautiful River. The English will be too late. They are slow. When they would move their settlers in, they will be stopped by French forts. They can do nothing. They have yet to cross the mountains, and we have only to go down the rivers."

"Yes, yes; but by what right do you enter the country of the Ohio, gentlemen?" stammered Jacob Vanbraam.

"By the discovery by our great La Salle sixty years ago,"

they babbled. "The Mississippi is ours and all the land watered by the rivers flowing into it. Huzzah! And what have the English? Nothing but their little colonies along the sea, bounded by the mountains. All west of the mountains, French."

"So you deny their claim to land west of the mountains?" Jacob Vanbraam queried.

"Yes, yes. What claim? A treaty with those Iroquois dogs who never owned the land to give; and who besides are rightful subjects of France and not of England! No, Monsieur the Captain—and you, Monsieur the Major: the banner of France is to float over all the country of the Ohio, and one year shall see it done, before you slow English in America can cut your trails."

"That will take many men, gentlemen."

"Bah! Fifteen hundred. They are waiting. We have a line of forts connecting us with Montreal, and supplies in store. We will meet our men and supplies coming up from New Orleans, and thus we will possess all the Ohio and the Mississippi. The Indians are joining France. You English cannot win the Indians. Already the Miami have sued for friendship."

"How is that?" Washington asked, through Captain Vanbraam.

"Certainly," prated Captain Joncaire. "The Miami have sent me two English scalps and a belt of wampum, for their French father, as token of their love. They see the strength of the French. The Delaware and Shawnee and even your Mingo Iroquois of the Allegheny have come to our camps and offered to help us march. The Sac, Potawatomi and Ojibwa are enrolled on our side. Just previous to your arrival here a band of Ottawa passed through with eight English scalps from below, for my commander their father. Oh, you can do nothing with the Indians. They are ours."

That was stunning news. The Miamis first had vowed friendship to Virginia and Pennsylvania; and now had turned around. Delawares, Shawnees, and even some of the Mingos (said Joncaire) were helping the French. And the Ottawas were on the war trail.

"But you are not drinking, Monsieur the Major,"

Joncaire continued. "The liquor of France is not to your liking?"

"The liquor may be excellent of the kind," Washington answered. "But I find the water excellent also."

Then one of the two other officers said something quickly, and Jacob Vanbraam as quickly translated again:

"He says you are too young and green to sit with men. You are a dolt."

But Washington made no reply.

So the others chattered again, and drank, and laughed, their tongues wagged, the smoke from their pipes formed a cloud; and amid the smoke, the chatter and the warmth the Hunter, well fed, dozed upon his bear-skin.

He roused, wakened by the scraping of the benches. This had signalled to him that Washington was going. The candles were low in their sockets, and the French and Washington and Jacob Vanbraam were upon their feet—the French swaying foolishly. Up scrambled Robert himself, throwing off his sleep.

"My thanks to you," Washington was saying, for Jacob Vanbraam to translate, "and my humble services. But I will sleep with my own men in my own camp, as befits a commander. I already have fared better than they." He turned about, and saw the Hunter. "You may stay and sleep by the fire, on account of your leg," he bade, with a sign.

"Yes, yes. Certainly," smiled Captain Joncaire, understanding the sign. And he said to Robert in French: "The poor little boy shall stay with his French brothers."

Robert shook his head. He was afraid of these French, so polite and so sure of themselves.

"I will go with Washington," he announced in English. "He is my captain."

When Vanbraam translated, the French laughed more loudly than ever, and Washington gravely smiled; and Robert followed him out into the cold blackness, for the camp in the woods.

IX
Half-King Causes Trouble

Things were going badly for Washington. This second day at Venango the rain poured down, so that the company could not start on. Tanacharison had learned from the Hunter all that had been said and done in Captain Joncaire's house. He and Juskakaka and White Thunder and Guyasuta were much impressed.

"The French," said White Thunder, "know what they are about. They are not afraid to talk right into the faces of the English. Now if they put the English out of the land, and we have helped the English, we shall have to pay."

"That is how it seems to me," said Green Grasshopper. "I am old, I have seen many things happen, and when the Indian helps in a quarrel he does well to help the stronger side. The white men are many. Let them fight, and we should wait till we know what to do. All we want is our land."

"The Governor of Virginia asked us to go with this Washington and we have come," said Tanacharison. "We made up our minds to give the speech belts back to the French who have treated us like bad children. We will do as we engaged to do. But I think it poor of Joncaire, who pretends to be our brother, to leave us in the woods and never send us anything to warm our stomachs. We are chiefs, as well as Washington who sits at the feast table while we stay in the rain with our speech belt. Washington says for us to beware of the French and their cunning words. But we are not children, we are men."

Washington had gone over to the house again, with Gist and Vanbraam. Pretty soon there came to the camp a lieutenant from Captain Joncaire. His name was La Force. He was a very lean, hungry-looking man, with yellow skin and staring, sly black eyes. He asked for the Half-King, and shook hands with him and Juskakaka, White Thunder and Guyasuta; and said to them, in their language:

"Captain Joncaire your brother is much hurt that you stay away from him. He has just heard that his brothers are here in the rain. He sends me at once to beg that his brothers will come in to his fire."

"Wah!" Half-King approved. "We will come."

So they all went with La Force; which was bad, too. Captain Joncaire gave them such a welcome, with his strong liquors, that they were made drunk, and did not return to camp this night.

Washington was disgusted. The French had them. But in the morning Tanacharison appeared, very sorry, when the camp was packing up.

"Now I am in my senses again," he said to Washington. "Wait a little, while I give the speech belt to these French."

"This is not the place for giving back the speech belt," replied Washington. "That man Joncaire is nobody. You will only waste time and we have no more time to waste. The place for delivering the speech belt is at the fort above, where you will see the head chief."

"No," said Tanacharison. "You are young, you do not understand. This place Venango is where the council fire with the French is kindled. I know Joncaire. He is the man to talk to. I ask you to hear what I say to him."

"Have done with your foolishness, then," answered Washington, growing angry. "But I tell you he will not accept the belt."

Just as Washington had warned, Captain Joncaire only listened, and refused the speech belt.

"It is a matter in which I am not concerned," he smiled. "My brother should carry the belt to the father at Fort Le Boeuf. But there is no hurry. The woods are cold and wet, and the fire at Venango is warm."

"We will start," said Washington, to Half-King.

"In a little," Tanacharison pleaded. "King Shingis has ordered Kustalogo the Delaware to deliver the Delaware speech belt, and I must find Kustalogo."

"That is nonsense," uttered John Davidson. "Kustalogo has told you he cannot make a speech for a king, and Shingis must deliver the belt himself."

Now if Tanacharison could only be got away from the presence of the French he would be all right. Washington did not dare to leave him or he would be made to believe lies, by the Kustalogo Delawares, and might be kept all winter by the French. He was a fine man, Tanacharison was, when he did not drink; but drink took his senses.

It was not until the morning of the fourth day that Washington at last succeeded in finding Half-King and the three other Mingos sober and ashamed. The march for Fort Le Boeuf began at noon. Captain Joncaire sent La Force and three soldiers to guard Washington by the best trail, and also to spy upon him.

The march up French Creek was even harder than the march from Logstown. By this time Robert's leg had healed nicely; but there was rain and sleet, marshes blocked the way, the crooked creek, icy cold, had to be crossed by swimming and wading. And the man La Force was constantly trying to frighten the Mingos by telling them of the Miamis and Delawares and Shawnees and of other Iroquois who had joined with the French.

Tanacharison did not listen; but all this—the wet, the cold, and the sly threats—Washington had to stand.

After seventy miles of winter travel, at nightfall of the fifth day from Venango, they sighted Fort Le Boeuf, at the head of French Creek.

There it lay, Fort Buffalo of the French, on the other side of the creek; and a powerful place it looked to be, rising from the snow and mud, half surrounded by a curve of the sullen stream, with the forest cleared to give it room, with its walls, twice a man's height, of flattened logs set on end, and sharp at the top, with great guns peeping through at the stumps and the water, with long barracks and many Indian lodges outside, and a host of canoes drawn up on the creek banks, waiting for spring; and the French flag above all.

While they of Washington's company forded the creek again, La Force went before to tell the fort who was coming. When, wet and muddy, they climbed out among the stumps, two officers of the fort came to meet them.

Then in the dark they entered through the big gate, where a soldier saluted. Camp was made. Wah! Here they were; but that had been a tough journey.

Evidently this was an important fort, and business should not be hurried. Washington was asked to wait until morning, when the commander would talk with him.

The officers here were very different from the crafty, blustering officers with Captain Joncaire; and the commanding chief, whose name was Chevalier Legardeur de Saint-Pierre, proved very different from the captain. He was a straight old man, with spick and span uniform, and medals, and with white hair, and only one eye, the other having been lost in battle.

He spoke a little English, and Washington spent a great deal of time with him and the under officers, after having delivered the letter from the Governor of Virginia.

But although they were good friends, it seemed, Washington was not blind.

"While I am busy," he said to Gist, "you have the Hunter count the canoes on the bank. He is a boy and nobody will notice him."

By knots in a string, one knot for every ten, Robert counted the canoes. There were fifty birch-bark canoes, and one hundred and seventy canoes of wood, besides many being built. In these the French were going to descend the creek and the river, in the spring. That meant a thousand men or more! Captain Joncaire had not lied.

The rains had changed to snow, and Washington was still waiting for an answer to the letter from the Governor of Virginia, so that he could start back. The horses were getting very poor, because there was little feed for them. On the third day he sent them off, with the packers, to Venango again.

"We will come down by canoe," he said, "which the French have agreed to furnish for us."

Then he told the Half-King to deliver the speech belt, and get that done with.

"Well," said the Half-King, "I have the belt, and when the head chief is ready I will give it to him. Let us not be in a hurry. You are young, but the chief and I are old and wise. Meanwhile you are being well treated and so am I. This place is a good place to stay, but the way home is long and cold."

There were other Indians and many half-breeds at the fort. They and even the French soldiers kept inviting Tanacharison, White Thunder, Juskakaka and Guyasuta to feasts, where much brandy flowed—a far better drink,

Tanacharison declared, than the rum of the English. So that all were kept half drunk, and their ears were filled with stories and warnings, and they were being urged to stay until spring at the fort where they would be comfortable among their brothers.

When the Half-King was in his senses he said he would not leave Washington; but when he was foolish he thought that he would stay and get more presents.

"I am going back," said Washington, angrily. "If your heart is good and you are a man you will deliver the belt at once. You are acting like a child and not like a chief, for these French plan to hold you."

"Wah!" uttered Tanacharison. "I am a chief. You are my brother. I will deliver the belt this very night."

That he did, in company with White Thunder and Juskakaka. The French commander and two other officers received them in private council, and listened to their words; but the commander would not take back the belt.

"My brother from the Indians of the Ohio is acting hastily," he answered. "Let him keep the belt which is the link of friendship from our father the King of France, until he hears again from me. He can rely upon his brothers the French, who wish only to live at peace with him. He has seen how strong the French are, and how generous. And as further proof of our love for our Indians of the Ohio, I am gathering together a present of goods, to be sent down at once to Logstown, that the Indian may not be poor. It is my request that you remain in my fort until the trail is open; then when you are rested and wish to go home you will find your people rich. I see your guns are rusty. In a day or two you shall have better guns, that you may hunt while you are here."

The speech pleased Tanacharison, but it did not please Washington, for the commander was smarter than the Half-King.

This same night the reply to the Governor of Virginia was received, and Washington gave notice that the start home would be made in the morning. Everybody knew, from the talk, that the Governor of Virginia had ordered the French out, and that the French refused to go out. They said again that the Ohio Country was theirs.

The canoes were ready, but Tanacharison would not go.

"It is impolite to leave so suddenly," he grumbled. "I ask Washington to wait one day, which will make little difference. The guns are promised us in the morning, and to run away from them would be like throwing dirt in the white-headed chief's face."

Washington turned red, but he kept cool.

"The white-headed chief says he does not know why you stay. He says you are free to leave; your business with him is done. If you want the guns, I will wait until morning. Then you must get your guns; and if you do not go with me I shall tell the Governor of Virginia, your father, that your hearts proved weak and you sold yourselves to the French for a bottle of brandy."

"Wah!" exclaimed Tanacharison. "Give me this day to get the drink out of us, and in the morning, after we have our guns that are promised, we will go at once with Washington."

This time the Half-King stood by his word. The French came with the guns in the morning, and with liquor, too, to "wet the present." Tanacharison took the guns, and reached out with his hand for the liquor. Then Washington, holding another gun, stepped between him and the liquor.

"Ask him," Washington said to John Davidson, "whether his tongue was drunk or sober when he gave me his word."

Tanacharison turned his back and leaving the liquor he strode down to the canoes. Washington spoke to the Hunter.

"We waited for guns for Tanacharison, Juskakaka, White Thunder and Guyasuta, who have acted like children instead of like men. I heard nothing about a gun for you, who have acted like a man instead of a boy. So I have a gun for you, and here it is. You well deserve it."

Robert the Hunter took the gun from the hand of Major George Washington. He was prouder of that than of the panther claws. It was a splendid little gun; with it were powder-flask and bullet-pouch.

The men with the liquor had laughed and had called after Tanacharison, who paid no attention. That was the true Half-King, at last. So they all went down to the canoes. They got in and shoved off. From the fort the French officers waved, and a great gun boomed goodby.

Thus, they left wintry Fort Le Boeuf. Washington had done well. He had come through three hundred miles of rain and snow and forest trail; he had delivered his letter and got his answer, and had brought off all his men safe. The French had not outwitted him; he had opposed them with patience, and had learned much. Now he had only to go back with the answer and the news.

But the French had not given up.

There were two canoes: one for the Washington white men, one for the Tanacharison men. The Hunter sat with Washington, Jacob Vanbraam, Christopher Gist and John Davidson. Their canoe led, Tanacharison's followed. They had gone but a little way upon the swift current, when Washington spoke sharply:

"Look there! We must hurry. Signal the Indians to mend their pace and keep with us. Company is coming."

Four canoes with French and Indian paddlers had appeared around the bend behind. They were loaded high. The loads, of course, were liquor, powder, lead and other presents for the Half-King party, and for Logstown, from the French "father."

"Yah!" said Jacob Vanbraam. "It is better not to let dem rascals camp with us."

"Or to get to Venango and below ahead of us," Washington added. "They will make mischief."

X

THE LONG DANGER MARCH

Gist and John Davidson were the paddlers; but the current of French Creek was so swift that they had to drop the paddles and use poles to fend off from the rocks and snags. The afternoon was cloudy and bitter cold. Upon either side of the black creek the snowy forest reeled in reverse.

The day was Sunday, December 16, said Washington. This evening, after sixteen miles of headlong, crooked course down the silent creek, camp was made. But Tanacharison passed by. The French canoes were not in sight, so that was all right.

The next day they found Half-King in camp below with Juskakaka and White Thunder.

"You are not travelling," Washington accused.

"No," said Tanacharison. "Guyasuta is out hunting and we cannot leave him."

"I think you wait for the French canoes and their liquor," answered Washington. The lines in his thin face had deepened; he looked worried again. "You see the water is falling, and ice forms. You know I have to go on, with my letter for the governor. Will you let the French steal your brains again?"

"Washington may go on. We will follow as soon as Guyasuta comes, but for the French we care nothing," declared Tanacharison.

After this it was see-saw—a race for Venango, where the horses waited. And ever the cold tightened, and the ice increased, and the creek grew shallower. Its channel was blocked, and they were obliged to get out and wade and carry the canoe around, from open stretch to open stretch.

First the French canoes passed, together with the Half-King's canoe. Now there were only three French canoes; one, loaded with presents of powder and lead, had been upset and lost.

Then they overtook the French canoes, and camped ahead of them and Tanacharison.

Gist And John Davidson Were The Paddlers

Then they came to rapids, of icy rocks and foaming water. From the bows Gist called back to Washington:

"Another carry, major, else we'll break our necks. The French are behind. Let them go through if they like it."

Once again they all stepped out, into water waist high,

and unloaded the canoe, and packed it and the supplies across a rough, slippery point of land, to the foot of the rapids. How quickly their clothing froze, while they stood to watch the French canoes, and Tanacharison's, sweep down, with thrust of pole and paddle to hold steady!

The canoes dashed in. They were flung to and fro. Would they make it? Yes! No? Look!

"Hah!" cried Gist. "As I thought. But they're getting out. All right."

"Huzzah!" Jacob Vanbraam cheered. "Dat is goot, very goot!"

"Good indeed," said Washington. "The cargo of liquor, wasn't it? Now it's safe in the creek, and we're rid of it in time." He looked well pleased.

For the canoe bearing the liquor had capsized near the foot of the rapids, and the crew were scrambling to the bank.

The other French canoes landed, to rescue the men. Tanacharison's canoe sped on; and Washington's men tumbled aboard their own canoe and pursued. This evening, when they went into Venango, never was a place more welcome, for after travelling seven days and more than one hundred miles by water, they were sheathed in ice from head to heels.

To be sure, there was liquor at Venango; but the liquor for Logstown had been lost, and this night Tanacharison, Juskakaka, White Thunder, and Guyasuta were too sick in the stomach to drink.

"You see," said Gist, "that the French tried to poison you with that stuff they sent by canoe. You will be wise to drink nothing here, and have nothing to do with this Captain Joncaire, or you may be poisoned again."

Half-King groaned. He could stand cold and wounds, but not cramps in the stomach.

In the morning Washington was ready to start on with the horses. He had sent Robert for Tanacharison.

"Now are you going with us by land, or do you wish to go by water?" he asked.

"White Thunder was thrown into the water and hurt," said Tanacharison. "He cannot walk, and he is sick besides. We think to stay here until he is better. Then we will take him down in a canoe."

"You are listening to Captain Joncaire," scolded Washington. "He would set you against the English. If you stay here you will get more drink and fine words, and when you have no mind the French will laugh over how they have fooled you."

That angered Tanacharison.

"What I am telling you is the truth," he said. "We wait for White Thunder. We shall not leave him among the French and he cannot ride upon a horse with you. Now I know the French. My eyes are open. They bewitched us with liquor which they pretended would be good for us, and they bewitched us with fine words. The liquor is out of our stomachs and the words are out of our ears. We are Washington men, and shall have nothing more to do with the French who work us only mischief. I put my hands between your hands, Washington, and when I meet you at the Forks of the Ohio I will give you a speech for our father the Governor of Virginia. And to show you that I am in earnest about the matter, I give you my son the Hunter to take with you. He will find you game; and if I prove untrue you shall keep him as my pledge. I hope that he will learn from you to be a great man. He has white blood in him."

"I will take him," answered Washington, "if he wishes to go." And he asked of Robert: "You have heard. Will you go with me to the white people of Virginia, and learn many things; or would you go with Tanacharison to Logstown?"

"I go with Washington to the Long Knife Americans," announced Robert.

"It will be a hard journey, through the winter."

"I go," said Robert.

"Here you could rest, and then travel by canoe to the people you know."

"I go," said Robert, "with George Washington."

Across the thin face of George Washington there glimmered one of those rare, grave smiles.

"We will come back to Logstown with an army to drive out the French," he said.

So Robert the Hunter, whose father was red, but whose mother was white, equipped like a warrior with his gun and his panther-claw necklace prepared to go with this George Washington whom he had grown to love as a strong man, a kind man, a man of patience and courage and great will.

"Will the Half-King be true, you think?" Washington queried.

"Yes," said the Hunter. "Tanacharison now sees that Washington is wise, and he has been foolish. The French would treat him as if he had no brains, he says; but the English are men and he will show that he is a chief. Tanacharison will always be your brother. When he tells Scarouady, Scarouady will be your brother, too."

By this time Washington's uniform coat and his trousers and his boots were worn out. He bought deerskin shirt, leggins, moccasins and a blanket coat from the Delawares at Venango for powder and ball, and changed to these.

The pack horses had rested, but they were too weak, still, to carry all the baggage. The packers had to ride, in order to drive the packs; but the other saddle horses, even Washington's, were loaded also. With Washington, Gist, John Davidson, Jacob Vanbraam (who was fat no longer), and Robert on foot, they all set out upon the winter trail again.

This proved slow work. The horses slipped upon the ice, they cut their legs in the snow crust and the frozen creeks, and had to be dug free of drifts; and after three days the party were only a little way out of Venango.

"This will never do," said Washington, tonight which was the night of the day called Christmas. "Gist, you and I will take what we can carry, in the morning, and make our best time ahead of the horses. Vanbraam will be left in charge to bring them on as he can, to Will's Creek."

"I'm afraid your feet will fail you, major," said Gist, "if you have no horse near for a lift now and then. They're sore already. You're more used to riding than walking with a pack on your back."

"I've been gone from the Governor almost two months, and have been six weeks in the wilderness," said Washington. "His Excellency will be getting anxious for the reply to his letter. Therefore I must make the best time I can in any way I can. We will take the Hunter, and go."

Early in the morning, after breakfast, they got ready.

Washington and Gist put on dry socks, tucked their leggins inside, pulled off their wet hunting shirts and tied their long woolen blanket coats about them, and Robert did much the same. Washington stowed his papers, wrapped in hide, in his pack of blanket and provisions, and slung the pack upon his back, and his gun upon his shoulders. Christopher Gist also shouldered pack and gun, and the Hunter had his own things.

Leaving Jacob Vanbraam with the other men and the horses they set on, through the lifeless, snow-laden forest, to reach the Ohio by the shortest way.

There was a little trail leading south. They followed this all day, in the snow and the cold, and had no water except by eating snow. Gist thought they might get to a place called Murthering Town, where some Delawares and Mingos lived; but after they had slipped and stumbled and ploughed for about twenty miles they came to an old Indian hunting cabin, standing empty in the dusk.

Washington was very tired. He limped on sore feet; and the Hunter could scarcely drag his legs.

"We'd better stop here, and eat in shelter and have a little rest, major," Gist said. "We can't reach Murthering Town before dark."

The logs and all were wet, and they ate without a fire, and lay down in their blankets. But Washington was impatient. As seemed to Robert he hardly had dropped off into a shivery doze when Gist and Washington were up, making ready to start on.

"We might as well move as freeze," Washington was saying.

Up staggered Robert. The night brooded coldly. Throughout the forest the limbs of the trees were cracking like gun shots. But the sky had cleared, so that when they hobbled out the black sky was sparkling with stars shining on the white snow. Washington looked at his watch and said it was two o'clock.

The sun was rising when they arrived at Murthering Town, and stopped to eat and get dry. The Delawares and Mingos of this town Robert did not know; they did not act very friendly, either.

"The French have been at work here," said Gist. "We'll

have no help from these people."

Pretty soon an Indian came to them, very friendly, and shook hands with Gist, saying in Mingo:

"Hallo, Oak-That-Travels," which was Gist's Indian name.

He shook hands with Washington, too, and sat down and began to talk.

"Watch out, major," Gist said to Washington. "This fellow's not to be trusted. He was at Venango when we went through, the first time. I remember his face."

"Brothers!" said the Indian. "The English are welcome. We see you travel on foot, and your moccasins are thin. You come from Venango?"

"Yes," answered Gist.

"Why do you travel on foot through the snow?"

"We travel ahead," said Gist.

"English do not travel on foot. They ride," said the Indian. "You have left your horses. My brothers were at Venango with horses. Are the horses on the way?"

"The horses will follow."

"If my brothers will tell us where the horses will be found, we will send out and bring them on by a short trail," said the Indian.

"He's plaguey curious," rapped Gist, to Major Washington. And he replied to the Indian: "We thank our brother, but the horses will know the way."

"Perhaps they will get here today, my brother thinks?" asked the Indian.

It was plain to Robert that the Indian was anxious to know where the remainder of the party were, with the horses and goods. Then Washington spoke up, to say to Gist:

"The fellow seems to know all about us, and we can't get away from him. It looks as though we'd been expected, by word from Venango. Ask him if he can guide us straight across country now, for the Forks of the Ohio."

"We'd do better to strike out alone, more into the south, major," Gist said. "Down this Beaver Creek, which will fetch us to the Ohio."

"No," said Washington, who was stubborn. "We lose time. I mean to cross at Shanopin's-town of the Forks and get into country that we know, on that side. The Governor is waiting on me."

The Indian acted very glad to show his brothers the way; and he had a hunting cabin, near water, in the east, where they all could stop for the night.

"Well," remarked Gist, "we're three and he's one, but I don't trust him. He's too friendly."

"It is not to my mind to show him we're afraid of him," answered Washington. "You may be mistaken in him. He speaks fair."

"He has a bad heart," suddenly said Robert. "Do not trust him, Washington. You can read his face."

"See? Even the boy knows," Gist laughed. "You have something to learn of Indians, yet, major. But we'll try him out."

The Indian put on snow shoes; and when he saw Washington limping and stumbling he stopped and took the pack.

"My brother the young chief is tired," he said. "I am strong. Now we will travel faster to my cabin, where we will rest again."

The Indian led up hill and down, through the woods, at a fast walk which made even the Hunter puff; and after they had gone ten miles Washington's legs wished to stop.

"We're veering too much to the north," he panted. "I can tell by the compass. Supposing we halt and get our bearings."

Gist and the Hunter were right willing to stop; and while Washington argued with the Indian in the sign language Gist said, to the Hunter:

"We must watch close. This fellow thinks evil." And Robert nodded.

The Indian did not like to stop.

"The young chief my brother is tired, so I will carry his gun too, for him," he said and tried to seize the gun. When Washington refused, the Indian grew angry.

"To camp in these woods is foolish," he complained. "Ottawas of the French are somewhere about. While we sit in camp they will take our scalps. We will be safe in my cabin."

"Where is your cabin now?" Gist asked.

"It is one gun-shot sound from here."

"Tell him to lead on, then," Washington bade. "But I'm beginning to think he means mischief."

The Indian led on for two miles, always trending more northward; and in two miles they had not reached the cabin.

"Wait. Where is the cabin. Have you lost it?" Gist called.

"It is two whoops. Let my brothers follow."

They did follow, for another two miles. The Hunter's feet were heavy like lead, and his moccasins were soaked through and through. Washington stumbled and slipped, and climbed the hills bent away over as if he had no stomach and could scarcely stand.

The Indian kept pausing, and waiting for them to catch up with him. Then Washington panted:

"This is all nonsense, Gist. The sun is low, that Indian has no cabin, he is lying. We'll camp at the next water, and make our own trail in the morning."

"I'll tell him to take us to water," answered Gist.

The forest had been thick and silent, with never a game track in the snow. But presently it opened to a fine meadow, of long grass weighted down by the snow, and here and there a great, naked oak tree. The sun had set red in the west; but the light from the sky made the meadow pink, and the snow, freezing again after having softened, crashed under foot and cut one's moccasins.

They were crossing the meadow, and making a great noise, with Washington bravely toiling along beside Christopher Gist, as if determined upon a good finish, and with Robert the Hunter behind, trying to step in their tracks, when on a sudden the meadow and the woods around it echoed to a ringing "Bang!" and a ball hissed past Robert's ear, and whined on.

The Indian had turned about, the smoke was oozing from his gun muzzle and the butt was still to his shoulder. From fifteen paces he had fired at Washington or at Gist.

Washington had stopped short.

"Are you shot, Gist?" he cried.

"No," answered Gist. "Did the beggar fire upon us?"

"I think he did."

"I'll have his hair for that!" said Gist.

The Indian was running. He sprang behind an oak tree,

and was loading. Gist threw off his pack and cocking his rifle was right after—feeling for his tomahawk as he ran.

Washington ran too, as best he could.

"Wait! Let him be a minute," he shouted. "Till we see what he does next."

They stood one at either side of the Indian, watching.

"If he puts in ball," said Gist, "his heart is bad. I'll crack him from here, major, or he'll do damage."

And Gist's gun was levelled and his finger upon the trigger.

"No," ordered Washington. Then he walked straight in, for the tree. "Give me that gun," he ordered. He looked at the Indian, and the Indian looked at him, and handed over the gun.

"The young chief is not angry with his brother?" the Indian asked. "His brother fires only powder, to clean his gun."

"Then why did my brother run behind a tree?"

"He was afraid. The white men did not seem to understand."

Washington drew the ramrod and dropped it into the barrel, and measured. Anybody could see that there was a ball on top the powder now.

"You ought to have let me kill him, major," said Gist. "He deserved death for that trick. Now we must keep charge of the guns, and get rid of him first chance we have."

They all went on, and came to a little stream. The sky had darkened, and the stars were out, and the forest was commencing to crack again.

"We will sleep here," Gist said to the Indian. "Make us a little fire to sleep by. You were lost, and you fired your gun so that somebody would hear?"

"Fire my gun to clean him," replied the Indian. "I know where my cabin is. Not far now. You come?"

"We will come in the morning," Gist said. "Tonight we are too tired. You travel on, with this cake of bread; and in the morning we will follow your tracks, and we hope you will have some meat to give us, at your cabin."

"That is good," agreed the Indian. "Let my brothers rest by the fire. When they come to my cabin in the morning they will find deer meat to show them I am their friend."

He went off, travelling fast among the trees.

"Be ready to leave at once when I'm back," said Gist; and he, too, went off, trailing the Indian.

"That Indian meant to kill one of us, Hunter," spoke Washington, as he sat with his feet to the fire.

"Yes," Robert answered. "I hear bullet whistle. He French Injun. Now he goes to tell other French Injuns."

"So I think myself," said Washington. "We'll have to clear out and keep ahead of them. Can you travel again in the dark?"

"A strong heart does not notice weak feet," said Robert. "I am a warrior, and can go where Americans go."

"You are half white, too."

"Yes. White blood go where Injun blood can go. Injun blood go where white blood can go. So I all go."

And Washington almost laughed.

They did not have long to rest. Christopher Gist came hurrying back.

"The fellow has no cabin. I trailed him a mile. We ought to start right on, major. He's making a straight course, and he'll have a pack of the red rascals upon us. I've no doubt there are Ottawas hereabouts, or as bad; and within gun shot, too. I didn't like the looks we got at Murthering Town, either. So we travel all night, or we're like to lose our hair."

"Very well," Washington answered; and he staggered up. "You lead, or shall I?"

"Turn about," said Gist. "First we'll go a little way and make a larger fire. They'll think we've only changed camps."

A large fire was built about half a mile on. It lighted up the woods, and looked very cosy; but they could not stay beside it. It was only a blind. So Washington read his compass, and took direction, and he led; then he struck flint and steel, to take direction again, and by the compass Gist led. In this way they travelled, southeast for the Forks of the Ohio, while the stars glittered and the branches snapped with the frost, and the wolves howled, until daylight.

But they had left a plain trail in the snow; and now by daylight the enemy would follow at full speed; so they three did not dare to camp. They ate bread and meat while they walked. Gist said that a little creek here ought to flow into the Allegheny. Down along the creek they plodded, all this day, without sleep. Surely Washington and Gist were strong men. Robert resolved that Tanacharison should hear about this march.

"We can go no further," gasped Christopher Gist, at dusk. "We'll camp where we are. I think we're safe until morning."

"And where are we?" George Washington queried.

"The creek has broadened. The Allegheny's within easy distance. We'll strike it at daybreak and cross on the ice."

"Once across, we'll soon be at Fraser's house and get horses," Washington planned. "Then I can make quick time to Will's Creek and on to the settlements."

They slept this night under a lean-to of boughs, their feet to a little fire. To sleep was very good. Never in his life had the Hunter been so fagged. They had walked with scarcely a pause a half day, a night and a day, through snow and upon ice, in sun, darkness and cold, up hill and down, ever in a wilderness.

Washington and Gist were astir early, ere the sky had lightened. Truly, Indians who would catch these two men should travel like the elk.

"Forward, march!" bade Major Washington. "Come, Hunter. We cross the river."

He hobbled, Gist hobbled, and Robert the Hunter hobbled after.

It was not far to the river. Robert had fallen a little behind when Washington, in the lead, halted stock still in the fringe of the woods. His voice carried clearly through the dawn light:

"Here's the river, Gist; but we're cut off. The channel's open."

XI

Facing Winter Peril

Christopher Gist hurried on. When the Hunter arrived, the two were gazing perplexed; and no wonder.

Here lay the swift Allegheny River, a quarter of a mile wide, but it was not frozen over. It was frozen for only fifty paces out from either bank. All the space between the borders was black current, in which great ice cakes, borne rapidly, churned and swirled on their way to the Forks below.

As far up and down as they could see there was no ice bridge—no way to cross afoot. To leap from floe to floe amid that mad race of tilting, spinning cakes, some thick, some thin, at intervals irregular, was impossible. And to swim through was impossible.

"Pshaw!" Gist uttered. "Who'd ha' thought this? In all reason the pesky river should be frozen clean across. We're cut short, major."

"Just where are we?" asked Washington.

"Maybe the boy knows better than we do."

"Shanopin-town across about two miles down," said Robert. "Forks another two miles."

"We'll have to go down stream, major," spoke Gist. "Until we come to an ice jam that will bear us, or can signal from opposite Shanopin's-town. The Injuns might be able to get a canoe to us. We'll find food and proper rest, too."

"No," said Washington. "The French spies are probably ahead of us. I'll not risk interference from Shanopin's-town—I must get to the Governor at all hazard. The less we see of Indians, the better. I have no time to take my ease. Cross here I shall."

"How so, then?" Gist asked.

"By raft. We'll make a raft and chance it."

Christopher Gist exclaimed:

"What! You mean to chance a raft in that ice, major? We're like to be swamped."

"It can be done, Gist. It's got to be done. Let's set to work."

"And that's a job, too," quoth Gist; "with only my hatchet and our hunting knives to shape the timber. But if you say so, I'm not the man to back out. Grant that the Injuns give us time."

"To work, then," bade Washington. "Keep an eye on our back trail and our guns ready. All I ask is time to cross."

They fell to, the three of them; and a job that was, to make a raft that would hold together and bear three persons. Saplings had to be cut down and trimmed with the one small hatchet; driftwood had to be gathered from along the steep, high banks; and all had to be laid closely and bound by poles fastened with wooden pegs.

Washington chopped, Gist hacked and laid and bound, the Hunter hauled and dragged; and while they toiled and sweated the sun rose higher until it marked noon.

The raft was not half completed. The driftwood was frozen and heavy, the saplings rang under the hatchet strokes. Gist had much difficulty in driving the pins that held the binders. They all needs must cast many an anxious glance upon the back trail, and upon the country up stream and down stream and across. Ever the floes whirled past, with no sign of lessening, nor of jamming.

The sun was sinking into the red west. A whole long day had been spent when Gist said, straightening to ease his tired back:

"She'll do, I think. It's the best we can manage, anyway; if we're going to cross before dark we'll have to make the try, major, or will you wait 'till morning?"

"We'll cross at once," declared Washington, "and be ready to march. We can sleep on the other side as well as on this side. Don't forget the setting poles. Here they are. Now to launch the thing."

The cumbersome raft weighed tremendously. They all bent to, and shoving, tugging, hoisting, they got it down a shelving place of the bank and upon the ice.

The ice creaked warningly, but held. The sun had sunk into the western forest. The air chilled suddenly and their sweat froze. The night was going to be clear and very cold.

To drag the raft over the snowy ice took time, for the footing was slippery to smooth moccasins. But at last the black water, washing the ragged ice fringe, was close before. One more shove—heave-o! The current and the speeding floes made a dizzy sight—the ice under sole cracked—the raft slid to the edge, and hung, half in, half out——

"Aboard with the Hunter!" cried Washington. "Quick!"

And Robert, his heart thumping, was alone, crouched upon the canted raft.

"Together, now, Gist! Jump as she enters."

They two strained—the raft slid in—Gist sprang—with final shove Washington gave a running jump, and landed; Gist thrust with his setting pole and out they went, careening into the wild mill.

There was one breathless moment; but the raft held, while the water seeped up through the crevices. It began to drift down stream at astonishing pace. Now Washington and Gist worked desperately with their setting poles, pushing the cakes aside, forcing the raft ahead, making way through the labyrinth that constantly closed and opened.

The drift was alarmingly rapid. Huge cakes blocked the trail, and others rammed them, threatening to bear them under. But they were creeping on, creeping on; they were half way. And now another floe swung athwart the course, and hung, so that the raft tilted while the current dragged at it.

Washington panted:

"Wait, Gist, till I pry off."

He bent to his setting pole, buried almost to the hand-hold in the water, to thrust the raft free. Then Gist cried out:

"Take care, major! No! He's gone!"

The raft had moved, the pole had been whipped from Washington's grasp, and losing balance he had plunged head first into the icy depths.

Gist sprang, Robert the Hunter sprang. An instant more, and Washington's head appeared just below the raft.

"Here, major!"

The water there was clear of floes. He swam a few strokes, and managed to grab the edge of the raft. With the raft canted dangerously again they hauled at him and he kicked and scrambled, and dripping wet he came aboard. Wah, but that had been a narrow escape!

"I lost my pole," he gasped.

"No matter," said Gist. "Thank Heaven you got out. But we can't make it tonight, major. We'll be wedged fast, and freeze to death. The best we can do is to land on that little island right ahead and build a fire."

Already they had been carried down stream a mile; in the gloom a bare little island, cloaked with only a few trees, cut them off from the farther shore. The raft drifted in to it, while Gist worked with his pole.

"When it touches, jump," he bade. "I can't hold it long."

The raft grated against the edge of the ice that bordered the island; pitching their packs out they all followed, leaping over the piled-up cakes; and away floated the raft. They were prisoners, but they had escaped the greedy river.

Nevertheless, it was a bad fix. The first thing to do was to build a rousing fire. Washington's teeth chattered and his clothing rasped as he moved briskly, to keep from freezing. The night was due to be the coldest yet.

It proved a bare little island indeed, of scarcely any brush, and with only two or three trees, and the highest part was not much above the river.

"There should be drift wood lodged at the upper end," said Washington. So he and Robert went seeking, while Gist started a fire of twigs. Luckily they found drift wood in plenty heaped against the island's head.

They lugged back snags and bark, to where Gist was blowing at his smudge. It seemed as though the fire would never burst into steady blaze, so damp was the wood, soaked with frost. Meanwhile Washington stamped and thrashed, but complained by not a word, save to say:

"We should have been across, except for my clumsiness. With two poles we would have forced passage."

"Not so, major," replied Gist. "Rather, be thankful that we escaped with your life. I confess I'd rather be upon the shore, myself. We're within rifle shot of it, without cover; and by daylight anybody could make things lively for us."

"Liveliness would do us no harm," laughed Washington. "It would warm us up. A possible skirmish bothers me less than the thought of delay. The Governor is waiting to hear of my trip. He sent me, instead of an older man, and he was criticized for it; so I would show that I am not one to fail."

The fire increased, lighting the island with its ruddy flare; but the cold increased, too, so that while they toasted one side of themselves, the other side chilled and stiffened.

"We dare not lie down, major," said Gist. "I can see you're ready to drop, and so is the boy; but if we lie down we'll sleep, and if we sleep we'll freeze to death. We must keep each other awake, and moving."

"Do you and the Hunter lie down, and I will watch and tend the fire," proposed Washington.

"No, sir," Gist objected. "You might drowse off— 'twould be only human nature to drowse off. Then, who would wake *you*? The boy may sleep, but we'll have to rouse him often or he'll be frostbitten."

"I am a warrior," declared the Hunter. "I will stay awake, and bring wood."

What a night that was! A still, stinging, cold night, while amid the stillness the ice boomed, the floes ground upon each other in the current, the forest cracked, the wet wood of the fire hissed, and overhead the million stars glittered in the black sky.

Now and then they three sat at the fire, or standing turned about to baste their backs; and to keep awake. Gist told stories of bears and Indians, and Robert told of his bear and the Cherokee, and Washington told of his plantation and of things to be seen among the Long Knives of the American settlements. When anybody felt drowsy he was made to walk, and rub his hands and cheeks with snow, or fetch more wood; and sometimes they roamed over the island.

"There's one advantage in this cold," said Gist: "The Injuns aren't likely to stir abroad before sun-up. But we may catch it if we're found here by the Ottawas."

"So you say," replied Washington. "You forget another advantage. The cold may bridge the stream for us, and we'll get off."

He was always hopeful, that man Washington.

Robert wearily trudged out again, for more wood from the drift pile. When he reached the spot, he stared, surprised. There, in the star-light, a log upon which he had stood high and dry, the last time, was being lapped by water. Wah! He ran back with the bad news.

"Washington! River comes up!"

The two men exclaimed.

"What? No!" "You can see."

And leaving the fire, see they did, at the drift pile, and also along the island edges. They set a stake and watched that; and the water crept higher.

"Either a gorge above has broken, or one has formed just below," said Washington.

"'Twill take little more rise to flood us off," remarked Gist. "I say things can't be worse."

"If they can't be worse they're ripe to mend," Washington answered steadily. "When we can't stay on the island we'll swim ashore, for we'll have to do something."

They all watched the stake. After midnight, by the stars, the water stopped, short of the fire, but the drift-wood pile was out of reach, except by wading. And that fear of being swept away by the black flood in the night was terrible—although it did not seem to worry Washington.

The stars slowly paled, and the east grew red. Washington returned from another trip to look at the channel between the island and the shore.

"The ice has packed, Gist!" he almost shouted. "Huzzah! We'll be able to cross. Thanks for the cold, after all."

His haggard face beamed.

"Aye," said Gist. "Then we'll make over as soon as we can, major, for I don't like these winter quarters. I've frozen all my fingers and some of my toes during the night."

"They should be tended to, sir."

"And so they will be, but you should deliver your message to the Governor. That is of first importance. Will the ice bear us?"

"We can try. Follow us, Hunter. If it bears us it will bear you."

They shouldered their stiff packs again, and rifles in hand went hopping swiftly but gingerly from stationary floe to stationary floe; and sprang to snowy land.

Thus ended the dreadful night.

The morning was steely cold, as yet. Once safe from pursuit, in the forest of this the east side of the Allegheny they stopped and made another fire, and ate, and each slept an hour while the two others fed the fire.

Now it was queer how comfortable and happy they felt, although it still was one hundred and forty miles to Will's Creek, and one hundred more to the place Washington called "home." But they had conquered.

Robert the Hunter decided that Indians, even Scarouady and Tanacharison, would not have tried to cross that river. They would have waited. Upon that island Indians would have given up and have died. Gist himself, a strong man, had stopped at the river, and had wished to turn down. But George Washington had said: "We will cross," and cross they did, and here they were.

"You will never have tighter squeezes for life, major," Christopher Gist declared, as they all travelled on. "Bullet, drowning and freezing—I tell you, you narrowly escaped. You're reserved for better fate."

Washington was striding briskly, as if tired not a whit.

"Whether for better or worse I hope to be equal to it," he said. "But I never feared for a moment that we would not get through."

They reached Trader John Fraser's house beside the Monongahela, this evening.

"Hah," spoke Gist. "Indians, major."

"Mingo!" cried Robert. "I see somebody." And he ran aside, while Washington and Gist went into the house.

A party of Indians were gathered at the edge of the woods near the house. He had recognized the tall form of Scarouady.

"Hallo, Scarouady."

Scarouady looked him over.

"I see the Hunter. But the Hunter is thin and hard. He is no longer a boy; he carries a gun and wears the panther claws of a warrior. Wah!"

"I have been far," said the Hunter.

"To the French."

"Yes."

"Where do you go now?"

"I go with Washington," Robert explained proudly. "I am a Washington man and go with him to the Washington Americans."

"Tell me," Scarouady bade. "I will listen."

When the Hunter had finished, Scarouady nodded gravely.

"Wah! You have done well. I see that Washington is a travelling buffalo, whom nothing stops. His name truly is Connotaucarius, the Eater of Land. The Great Spirit protects him so that he may lead the Long Knife Americans upon the war trail. It is time that the great house with guns and goods be built at the Forks of the Ohio, for the French will come soon. You tell Washington that when he marches against the French, Scarouady will bring warriors and help. Goodby."

"You are going?" asked the Hunter.

"We stay tonight at Queen Allaquippa's town. Tomorrow I will talk with Tanacharison at Logstown and learn what he knows."

"Where have you been, Scarouady?"

"To get scalps in the Catawba and Cherokee country. When we were part way we found five Englishmen and two English women lying dead in some houses. The tracks were Ottawa tracks; but for fear the English would think we had done it and would attack us we turned back, to tell Fraser."

Scarouady and his nineteen warriors left, up river to visit Queen Allaquippa's town, three miles away. Wah! So the Ottawas of the French were raiding even far into the south! Washington had struck to the eastward none too rapidly.

Now the road to Assaragoa the Governor of Virginia was open, although still long. While John Fraser was trying to find horses, Washington wrote his travel story in his book.

Queen Allaquippa sent word that she was offended because Washington did not visit her. They went to see her, the next day, and he gave her his red blanket-coat, which pleased her.

"I heard you passed me by once, which was impolite," said old Allaquippa, woman sachem of the Delawares, who was fat and wrinkled and smoked a pipe. "You probably were in a hurry. But now I think well of you. I am a lonely widow with two sons, and should have a husband to protect me from the French. Is Washington supplied with wives?"

"Hah! She wishes to marry you, major," Gist chuckled.

Major Washington turned red, and soon left as if he were glad to get away.

"That is your fourth narrow escape," Gist laughed again.

"Yes," Washington replied soberly. "A wife with a tomahawk at her belt is scarce to my liking."

Trader Fraser could find no horses. On this day called New Year's Day, of January 1, 1754, they three set out once more, on foot, for Christopher Gist's new place, southeast upon the way to Will's Creek. There they got horses.

"Within one week we shall be at the frontier of Will's Creek; in another week I shall be reporting to the Governor," said Washington, as from Gist's place they jogged on, in the rain, following Nemacolin's Trail through forest and mountains, with Will's Creek and the Ohio Company's store-house at the Potomac seventy miles distant.

"You will urge him to fortify the Ohio at once, before the French descend in the Spring?" Gist asked.

"I shall press upon him the instant need of a fort and trading-house in the Forks; the place that I am recommending in my report," answered Washington.

They made what haste they might, again, upon poor horses, in bad weather, over a heavy trail. Washington was eager to report to Assaragoa and have the French stopped; Gist's fingers and toes demanded medicines; and Robert the Hunter looked forward to strange sights in the towns of the Long Knives—he had been promised that he should shake the hand of the Long Knife Governor himself.

They had been travelling four days and were within one day's journey of Will's Creek, when they heard shouts and snappings. Then at a turn of the blazed trail they were face to face with a line of white men, a few ahorse and the others afoot, driving pack animals.

"Ho!" uttered Washington. "Whither bound?"

"To the Forks of the Ohio, sir."

XII
ROBERT CARRIES BAD NEWS

He was a fresh-complexioned young man in red uniform coat and red trousers buttoned into gaiters at the calf, and cocked hat, and wore a sword, like a soldier.

"On what business? I am Major George Washington of the Virginia militia."

"Your servant, sir," said the young man. "I am Ensign Edward Ward of Captain William Trent's company from the frontier, to establish a fort in our Ohio country beyond the Great Mountains. You are safe returned, Major Washington? What of the French? They will advance?"

"You will be first, sir, if you act boldly," Washington replied. "Is this a movement by the militia?"

"We are Independents, sent to protect the holdings of the Ohio Company along the Ohio."

"Where is Captain Trent?"

"Enlisting other men, to follow with cannon and powder. How far to the Forks, sir? You have been there?"

"I, and also Mr. Gist, whom you see. The Forks are one hundred and forty miles, by slow trail. But the principal fort should be located there, at all hazards," asserted Washington. "Spend no time in looking elsewhere. I am hurrying to the Governor with that advice."

"The Indians are to be friendly?" Ensign Ward queried. "Settlers are only one day behind me, to take up company land at the Monongahela."

"You have an interpreter with you?"

"Not yet, sir. We hope to meet up with the trader John Davidson, and employ him. But where, I do not know."

Washington replied quickly:

"He is coming with Captain Vanbraam and my pack horses, but their whereabouts are uncertain. An interpreter you should have. This boy will serve you. He is the adopted son of the Mingo Half-King at Logstown, and I vouch for him. He speaks English, and understands a little French. He will be of great help to you. His name is the Hunter, and a hunter he is, and knows the country. He has been all the way to the French with me, and has borne himself bravely."

Washington turned to Robert.

"I wish you to go with these men," he said gravely. "You are willing?"

A lump had risen in the Hunter's throat. He had travelled far, he had had a hard time, he was almost at the end of the trail in the comfortable country of Washington's Americans where he was to learn to be white—! So he hesitated for just a moment. Then he said:

"I will go. I am American."

"Bravo!" smiled Washington. "It is the part of an American to serve his country."

The Hunter gulped.

"You will come, Washington?"

"If I am honored with an appointment to the wilderness again, I will come."

"All right," said the Hunter. "I go to help keep the French out."

Washington and Gist rode on. Robert turned around, for the trail back to Dekanawida, and the Mingos and Delawares, and perhaps that Logstown which was nothing like the white towns described by Washington. Tanacharison would be surprised.

There were thirty men, and seventeen pack horses loaded with fort-building material and trading-house goods. The men did not look to be the equal of the French; they were not all soldiers—they seemed more to be traders and woodsmen, and were poor and ragged, and badly armed. The soldier captain, Ensign Ward, appeared to be not much older than Washington, but he was younger acting—he talked more and as they travelled he asked many questions of the Hunter, and often laughed.

They were a long time in getting the pack horses over the rough, narrow trail; across the Savage Mountains, and the Great or Alleghany Mountains, and the swollen, icy Youghiogheny or Four-Streams-in-One River, and through the Great Meadows, and across the Laurel Ridge to Gist's Place, and then on west to the Monongahela River at the mouth of Redstone Creek, where Nemacolin's Trail ended.

Here they had to stay and build the first storehouse for the Ohio Company. Captain William Trent (the same man who had failed to reach the French, before Washington was sent) arrived with more men, dressed in red, and with ten cannon in carts, and eighty barrels of powder and muskets.

It was the middle of February when the storehouse was finished. Trader John Fraser had come in and had been made a lieutenant; but he said that he would not act unless he had permission to attend to his trading business too. Then Captain Trent left, to go back to Will's Creek. A number of the men went, also, for they had grown tired. Lieutenant Fraser and Ensign Ward were told to march on and build the fort at the Forks, forty miles down the Monongahela. But Fraser stopped at his trading house, and after that they saw little of him; and when Ensign Ward reached the Forks he had only about forty men, and no great guns or powder.

While they were looking about for a good place for the fort, Tanacharison and White Thunder came up, to talk.

"I thought you were with Washington," Half-King said to the Hunter.

"I went with Washington nearly to the Long Knife settlements; then he ordered me back to talk for this man who is to build the fort," answered Robert.

"Who is this young man?"

"His name is Ward. He is the captain here."

"Wah!" grumbled Tanacharison. "I found Washington wise, but now Assaragoa sends us another boy without hair on his face. Where are the great guns?"

"They will come," said the Hunter.

"It is no use to build a fort without great guns," declared Half-King. "And spring is near. As soon as the waters are open the French will be here in numbers like the wild geese. I will talk with this boy."

Tanacharison talked with Ensign Ward, and liked him. Others from Logstown, and men from Shanopin's-town and from Shingis's town and from Allaquippa's town spent a great deal of time watching the fort grow; but it grew slowly.

John Davidson came from Will's Creek. He said that Washington was raising another company of soldiers, and would march as soon as they were ready.

The waters had opened. The floating ice in the Allegheny had almost cleared, and of the fort only a few log walls were up, to form a storehouse for the trading goods, and buildings for the soldiers, when close behind the ice there arrived the French.

They were four days distant, up river, when the first news of them was heard; and it was bad news, for the French were many, in many boats with cannon.

Ensign Ward sent a runner to tell Captain Trent at Will's Creek; and he sent the Hunter to bring Tanacharison and Scarouady for council.

"If you mean to fight off the French," said Tanacharison, "you should at once build a high fence, with a ditch, and stay behind it, where you can move about. Else you will be shut up in these little houses and the French will knock them to pieces over your heads with their great guns. Where is Fraser? He has more experience than you."

"I will get him," answered Ward. So he went up to John Fraser's trading place, eight or ten miles south; and Lieutenant Fraser said he could not leave his business—he knew that the French were near, and he did not see that anything could be done.

"Then I will build a stockade and wait; for I think it a shame to draw off before the French, as the rest of you have done," Ward answered angrily. "The Indians will think us cowards."

The men worked very hard, building a stockade of sharpened pickets, with a ditch inside it, in a good place. This last morning which was the morning of April 17th, White Thunder's pretty daughter Bright Lightning borrowed Robert's horse to ride up to Shanopin's-town. Nobody could refuse Bright Lightning anything.

"Maybe I will see the French," she said. "These English see nothing. They have no scouts out. I wish I were a warrior."

"Well, you can marry a Delaware and perhaps some day you will be a woman sachem like old Allaquippa, and smoke a pipe," Robert teased.

"Wah!" exclaimed Bright Lightning. "She is ugly and fat. When I tell you the French are coming, then I'll know whether you and your Long Knife Americans are warriors, yourselves."

Bright Lightning rode off astride. She had been gone only two hours when back she galloped——

Bright Lightning Rode Off Astride

"I have seen the French! The army of Onontio is near, in boats."

"Where?"

"Above Shanopin's-town. The boats are like leaves upon a stream in Falling Leaf month."

"If she speaks the truth, we will see," said Tanacharison. "If she does not speak the truth, she shall be punished, but there is no harm in finishing the stockade."

The Ward men worked harder than ever. They had just put up the gate that closed the last opening when, at noon, the French fleet did sweep around the bend at Shanopin's-town, two miles up the Allegheny.

It was the army from Fort Le Boeuf! Wah! How many? Almost four hundred boats, small and large, blue with soldiers and bristling with muskets!

The French made a fine landing at the Forks and marched right in, to halt beyond musket shot while an officer came on with a white flag and two Indians. He wished to talk. Taking Tanacharison and the Hunter, Ensign Ward went out from the stockade and met him.

The Indians were French Iroquois, named Owl and Two Drums. Owl spoke English, so that Robert had only to listen and know that his words were the true words.

"I am Captain de Mercier," said the officer, through Owl. "My commander the Chevalier de Contrecoeur directs that you retire at once with your men from this land belonging to the King of France; and by this belt of wampum he bids the Half-King, whom I see with you, do the same."

"And what if we decline?" answered Ensign Ward, standing bravely.

"You will suffer the consequences of your rashness," replied the French officer. "We will take possession just the same."

Looking past him they could see great guns being unloaded from the large boats and dragged in shore.

"I must have a little time to think," said Ensign Ward.

The French officer looked at his watch, and he said:

"It is near two o'clock. By three o'clock you must appear at my commander's camp with your reply in writing, or we shall proceed against your works."

Tanacharison broke into a rage and threw the wampum belt upon the ground.

"You tell your captain chief I do not know him. There is his belt. He has no rights here, to order me or the English what to do. This is not French land. It is Iroquois land, and my land. I invited the English to come upon it; I ordered a fort to be built and I laid the first log."

But the officer only turned upon his heel and strode away, together with Owl and Two Drums.

Ensign Ward, very red and walking stiffly, went back to the little stockade, where the men had been watching and waiting. It was plain to be seen that he did not know what reply to make. He showed good sense, though, for he held council with Tanacharison and Scarouady and White Thunder, who were older than he. The Hunter and John Davidson translated such words as might not be understood.

"I wish to know what you would do if you were in my place," he said, to Tanacharison. "I am alone here, with only forty men, of whom but thirty-three are armed. I have no cannon, and but little provisions for a long fight."

"The French number a thousand, with great guns," Half-King answered. "Where is your captain, with guns and men, that he does not come to help you?"

"I sent word to him four days ago," said Ensign Ward. "I know nothing about him."

"It is a strange thing in Assaragoa to put a handful of men under somebody of no experience in the midst of the woods and leave them to the French," declared White Thunder. "Where is Washington? He does not fear the French, but that man Trent has gone home a second time without even seeing the French."

"Do the Mingos tell me to fight the French, and that they will help?" Ensign Ward asked quickly.

"What does Scarouady say?" said Tanacharison.

"Wah!" replied Scarouady—he of the tattooed chest and cheeks. "Were we to fight the French we should have fought them on the river where they could not use their great guns. Then they would have turned back. To fight them now requires a council, and plans; and they have Iroquois brothers with them. That is how it seems to me."

"Listen," bade Half-King; and he spoke wisely: "The French may not wish to fight. If they fire and kill men, that means war with the King across the water. This is not Onontio's land; it is land given to the English for a fort, and the English are here first. To drive them off is war, but to talk is not war. Now I think that Ward should say to the French: 'I am only a small chief, put here to build a trading house upon land given by the Iroquois, and I know nothing of any wrong in the matter. So I cannot make answer without orders from my captain chief. But my captain chief will be here within a day or two, and he will talk with the French captain.'

"That is how Washington and I were treated at Venango and Fort Buffalo," continued Half-King. "The French will see that you are speaking the truth; and while they are waiting Washington will be coming, and he will attack them from behind while you fight them from in front."

"That's good sense," approved John Davidson.

This answer Ensign Ward decided to make, when the hour was up. Then Tanacharison took the Hunter aside.

"Quick!" he said. "We cannot depend on that man Trent. Do you set out on foot so you will not be seen; find Washington and give him this belt, and say to him: 'Your brother cries to you from the depths of his heart and bids you come at once to his assistance or we all are lost and may never meet again.' Tell that to Washington and to no other. He shall be our hope."

Robert the Hunter turned around and ran through the stockade, to get out by the back. Men would stop him with questions but he paid no heed, for the words of Tanacharison were repeating in his mind. He dived past the gate sentinel, and was outside, when somebody called. It was Bright Lightning running after.

"Wait! You are running away, Hunter?"

"Think so if you like," he answered. "Goodby."

"No," panted Bright Lightning. "You do not run away. You go to bring Washington. I guessed. Take this, for the long trail." And she handed him a piece of dried venison and a little bag of parched corn. "Hurry!"

And he hurried on, feeling grateful to Bright Lightning. She was a good girl. He would not tease her any more.

At first chance he plunged into the forest, upon shortest trail to Washington. Whether the French would let Ward stay, he did not know. Perhaps the Long Knives and the Mingos would try to fight the French—he could see that Tanacharison was much worried. This he did know: he had more than one hundred miles to travel, and the piece of meat and the parched corn would help him a great deal.

When on the evening of the fourth day from the Forks the Hunter trotted afoot down to the mouth of Will's Creek he was very tired and the belt about his stomach was very small; for he had slept little and his meat and parched corn were gone. He had stopped only to rest, and not to hunt. But that which he now saw gladdened his eyes.

Around the Ohio Company's log storehouse in the clearing along the Potomac where Will's Creek entered there were a large number of tents, and many men were moving about. It looked as though he had met Washington.

He panted in among the tents. The soldiers and other men, most of them poorly dressed and doing nothing, stared at him or laughed as if they thought him only an Indian boy coming to beg. And then he espied somebody he knew.

It was the fat Captain Vanbraam, of Dutch Land, who had been left behind on the trail from Venango last winter.

"Ho," cried Robert. "Vanbraam! See me."

"What iss?" answered Jacob Vanbraam. "Oh! Eh? Yah! It is our Injun boy again. Where you come from now? You want me?"

"I want Washington. Where is Washington?"

"Yes; Washington, of coorse. He is not to be boddered. Eh? What? You tired? Hungry? Somebody chase you?"

"I bring words," said Robert. "From Tanacharison. Where is Washington?"

"Oho!" quoth Jacob Vanbraam. "Den come along. I take you."

Captain Vanbraam strutted off with Robert at his heels; and saluting at the open flaps of a tent guarded by a soldier, said:

"Here is one to see you, colonel."

George Washington replied:

"Let him come in."

Washington, in red uniform, was sitting upon a stool at a little table, writing in the dusk; when he saw the Hunter he stood up—his eye was quick, he knew that something was the matter, for with tired face suddenly made hard and sharp he uttered:

"The Hunter! You've been travelling—you bring news?"

"Tanacharison says to Washington: 'Your brother cries from his heart to you to come quick and help us or all is lost and he may never see you again.'"

"What?" exclaimed Washington. "How's that? Where are you from?"

"The Forks. The French come, one thousand. Tanacharison send me for Washington."

"What did the French do? Where is Ensign Ward, who builds the fort?"

"Ward there. French there. Mebbe fight, mebbe not. French tell Ward to get out. Tanacharison say wait."

"Hah!" exclaimed Washington. "You hear, Vanbraam?"

"Yes; and two days ago we hear dat Captain Trent and all was captured by the French. Den when we arrive we find Trent at dis Will's Creek, and he knows nodding about it. He says he left Ward safe, and has no news. So what to belief? Mebbe all a scare."

"I trust this boy, sir," replied Washington.

"The word is true word," said Robert. "I see the French. They are there, Washington."

"When was it?" asked Jacob Vanbraam.

"Four days. I came straight."

"Impossible. It is one hoonderd and fifty miles, by bad trail in bad wedder," scoffed Jacob Vanbraam.

"I make own trail," said Robert.

"You look it. You are tired, hungry too," said Washington. "I thank the Hunter. Was the fort finished? Is it fallen?"

"Not finished. French say to go away in one hour. Tanacharison tell Ward to say he must wait for his chief."

"Summon the officers for a council in my tent immediately, captain," ordered Washington, of Vanbraam. "If the fort has surrendered we may expect Ward himself soon. The boy has evidently beaten any other messenger."

Then he called in a black servant, and the Hunter ate, and answered more questions, and lay down to sleep in George Washington's tent.

XIII
Battle And Victory

Washington was going! Everybody soon believed the Hunter's story, for Ensign Ward himself and his men came in. The French captain had not allowed him to wait, but had again ordered him off.

Tanacharison had sent Scarouady's son the Buck, and Guyasuta the warrior with Ward, bearing another cry for help. The Buck had gone on with Ward, to the Governor; and Guyasuta had travelled back to the Half-King with an answer from Washington.

"We thank you for your friendship and your wise counsels," Washington had said. "This young man will tell you that a small part of our army is marching toward you, clearing the road for our great guns and our supplies. I hope that you and Scarouady will meet me on the road as soon as possible to aid me with your advice. This string of wampum will remind you how much I am your brother and friend."

The French at the Forks numbered one thousand, by best count; Guyasuta asserted that six hundred Chippewas and Ottawas were marching south through the Miami country, to join another army of French coming up the Ohio River.

Washington had been waiting here at Will's Creek for pack horses that had been promised him. He ordered out sixty of his men to be widening and smoothing the Nemacolin Trail so that he could travel rapidly. But no pack horses were given him; so he found what wagons he could, and a few horses to draw them, and with the rest of his men, one hundred, he started. The Trent men would not march again, and had gone home.

His great guns had not come, either. The chief of all the Long Knife army being raised was Colonel Joshua Fry—the man who had talked for Virginia at the big council in Logstown summoned by Christopher Gist. Washington was second in command, and now Fry would follow with more men and the great guns. It seemed to Robert that for Washington to go against those many French and Indians in the woods, with only a company and a half, mostly ragged traders and settlers called "raw" (whatever that meant) by Jacob Vanbraam, was foolish.

But they were Long Knife Americans, and good shots, and Washington commanded. He had with him Jacob Vanbraam, and one Peyroney a French American, and several others who looked to be skilled warriors, for his officers; and with Tanacharison's help maybe everything would be all right.

Anyway, he was going first to the mouth of Redstone Creek, where at the end of Nemacolin's Trail the Trent men had built the trading house, and he would wait there for Colonel Fry and the great guns, before attacking the French.

Now again it was a hard march over the Savage Mountains, and over the Alleghany or Great Mountains, and across the Youghiogheny or Four Streams-in-One River, and through the Great Meadows and over the Laurel Hills, and past Gist's place, to Redstone Creek at the Monongahela.

The sixty men sent ahead had been able to do little with the road; the horses for the baggage wagons soon gave out, and the men had to drag the wagons, themselves; so that after a week Washington was no further than Little Meadows, twenty or twenty-five miles from Will's Creek.

The news was bad, brought by traders driven out by the French. The French had built a strong fort at the Forks. They had increased by eight hundred soldiers, and six hundred more soldiers were coming up the Ohio! One trader had met the French officer La Force and four French soldiers, from the Forks, scouting around Gist's place and spying out the country. The French were buying the Delawares, Shawnees and Mingos with presents. But Tanacharison, said the trader, was marching with fifty warriors to join Washington; and that was good news.

As he marched, Washington left behind him a road smoothed for wheels, so that the great guns could be brought on swiftly. Therefore his march was slow. When he was forty miles from Will's Creek the Buck met him, with fresh word from Tanacharison.

"The French army is coming to find Washington," were the words now carried by the Buck. "Let Washington be on his guard against them. They intend to strike the first English that they meet. They have been on the march two days, but I do not know their number. I and my chiefs will be with Washington in five days."

"Where is Half-King?" Washington asked.

"He is watching the French until his people get their corn planted."

"What are the French at the Forks doing, then? Is it true that more men come in to them?"

"No," said the Buck. "They are the same that made my brother the soldier Ward go away. But they have raised a fort with walls as thick as a man is tall, and have pointed their great guns at the woods and the river."

"I ask you to go back and tell Half-King that you saw me," said Washington. "I shall march on to the Great Meadows, and build a little fort, and wait the French. Tanacharison will find me there."

The Great Meadows were eleven miles on across the swift Youghiogheny. The Washington men began to clear away the bushes and dig a ditch, and scouting parties searched about for the French.

"I t'ink dere is no French," said Jacob Vanbraam. "Except at the Forks, where by most reliable report dey haf no more dan fife hoonderd to eight hoonderd men. Bah! Are we children, to be frightened by big talk?"

Then, late in the morning, Christopher Gist rode into camp from his place twelve or thirteen miles north, beyond the Laurel Hills. He must have had fresh news of the French, for very soon half the men, led by Ensign Peyroney, hastened out, as to war; and next Washington's soldier messenger told the Hunter to come to Washington, quick.

"Listen, Hunter," spoke Washington: "You shall find Tanacharison, who is coming, near Gist's place, and bring him to me. But tell him to be very careful, for the French are at hand. Gist says the man La Force and fifty French were at his house yesterday while he was gone, and today he saw their tracks made in the night five miles from his place. I have sent men to chase these French; and if Tanacharison will come maybe we shall catch them. Do you be careful, too, that they don't catch you."

"They not catch me," declared Robert. "I will be Indian."

The day was rainy and dark. Robert the Hunter hastened out, to find Tanacharison. It would not do to take the little trader's trail leading northeast over the Laurel Hills, for no doubt the French spies were lurking along it. Besides, Tanacharison, 'twas said, had moved from Logstown to the Monongahela south of the Forks, to plant corn in a place safe from the French soldiers.

Therefore the Hunter made his own trail; and travelling his best he struck the Monongahela, flowing leaden under the leaden sky; and after a long time he discovered the new and muddy cornfields of the Mingos, skirted by rude shelters from the weather.

Now it was afternoon, but no Tanacharison was here, nor was anybody here except women and a guard of a few old men.

"Tanacharison is gone," they said. They were in bad humor. "What do you want of Tanacharison, boy? If you pretend to be a warrior instead of a white runaway you can follow his tracks and find him, but our business is to plant corn so we won't starve while the French and the English are fighting."

Old Juskakaka or Green Grasshopper was lying in his brush hut, sore with rheumatism. He scowled.

"Tanacharison is spying on the French," said Juskakaka. "He took men and marched east this morning. He will do better to let the French alone and stay friends with them. The French are fortifying everywhere; the woods are full of their soldiers; and when they have whipped the English they will not bother the Mingo. You will be wise to wait for Tanacharison here. He may not thank you for chasing him up with trouble words from Washington who has only a few men and knows little of fighting."

"I shall find Tanacharison," said the Hunter, much to old Green Grasshopper's disgust.

He circled out, like a dog, searching the ground; and finally he did come upon a warrior trail washed by the day's rain. Wah! That was it. It pointed east, into the forest; and into the forest again plunged Robert the Hunter, using all his wits. He had been sent to find Tanacharison.

Now the trail proved to be long, as if the warriors had travelled rapidly; and it was cold and thin and hard to see; and the gloomy forest darkened with drizzle and early night, and the Hunter was tired and hungry when suddenly an Indian sprang up beside him.

And that was Scarouady. Ho!

Scarouady, in full war paint, had been lying like a panther beside the trail. He said severely:

"What do you do here alone in the woods, carrying your scalp in your hand?"

"I bear word from Washington to Tanacharison," panted Robert. "The French are near."

"That is no news," Scarouady grumbled. "But come. The trail needs no more watching."

The Hunter did not know where he was, exactly, until he had followed Scarouady to the warrior camp. This was in the lee of Big Rock—a high ledge upon the south slope of Laurel Hill. He had circled almost back to the Great Meadows.

Tanacharison and five or six Mingo warriors were sitting around a little fire that hissed in the pelting rain. The night promised to be bad.

Half-King listened to the word from Washington.

"Very well," he said. "Maybe the English are going to do something at last. You wait here and eat and rest. The Buck and Guyasuta are out upon the fresh tracks of two French. We want to hear what they have to say."

It was a miserable wait. The rain grew worse, the wind moaned, and the fire against the rock flared and sputtered. There were French somewhere near, preparing to attack Washington. Everybody knew that. Whether they would move in the rain, or would try to hide, had to be found out.

Half-King, and White Thunder (who was here) and the others, were in Mingo war-paint, like Scarouady. That looked serious. Sitting, the Hunter fished into the little hide sack that he carried inside his shirt, and he, too, daubed his cheeks with vermilion. He had told Washington that he would be Indian again; and now Indian he was.

Then, after what seemed like another long time, without any warning sound two figures suddenly stepped from the dark into the fire-light. They were the Buck and Guyasuta, with rain-water running down their painted faces.

They sat. Pretty soon Half-King said:

"Guyasuta may tell us what he and the Buck found."

"We followed the back trail of the two men and found where they came from," reported Guyasuta. "They came from a company. The company will be camped not far away. We think it is the same company that was spying near Gist's place."

Tanacharison did not speak, for a minute. He was making up his mind. Then he said:

"You are right. The two men are going to the fort at the Forks. The company will wait till they return. If the English wish to fight, now is the time." And he said to Robert: "You go back to Washington. Tell him his brothers the Mingo know where fifty of the French are, getting ready to strike him. Let him come here at once, with his men. We will show him how to surprise the French before they grow greater in number, for they have sent off two men whose tracks we have seen."

Out went Robert, into the dark and rain. The camp of Washington in the Great Meadows was no distance at all, by day; he should have reached it in an hour; but to find it tonight was a very different matter. Before he saw its candles glimmer through the wet blackness he feared that he had lost it.

He did not waste any time with the sentries—he slipped through the lines without being hailed and was at Washington's tent.

Washington was talking with John Davidson the trader. He listened gravely to the message from Tanacharison. Then his blue eyes glowed. He seemed glad. He folded his letter and fastened it and called a soldier and said: "Have this started to Governor Dinwiddie at once in the morning." And now, to Robert:

"Where is the Half-King?"

"At Big Rock. He waits for Washington."

"And how far is Big Rock?"

"Not far. Half way to Gist's place. One hour ride, two hour walk."

"Do you know, Davidson?" Washington asked.

"Big Rock is an Injun camp spot near where the trail to

Gist's crosses the crest of Laurel Hill, colonel," said John Davidson. "About six miles from here."

"We could find it speedily?"

"Not till morning. The night's pitch dark, the trail's bad at its best and by night in this weather is no trail at all. You can be sure that the French will stay snug while you do the same."

"Then all the more reason to move against them, sir," Washington answered. "They fancy themselves safe. I'll not have our Indian allies say that when they sent for us with urgent call we preferred comfort to action. We will go at once."

"I will show the way," said Robert. "Maybe take a long time, but we find Tanacharison."

"Well spoken," Washington praised. "The Hunter came, he can go back."

"We'll need Indian senses, that's sure, colonel," laughed John Davidson. "You see the boy's got his war paint on."

"Maybe Injun now, but American too," announced Robert.

Washington smiled.

"You may rest while the soldiers are getting ready. How many men has Tanacharison?"

"Scarouady there; White Thunder, Guyasuta, Aroas, Buck, two-three more."

It was an hour before they all set off—Washington himself, and forty men, and Robert the Hunter as guide. Captain Vanbraam was left with the other men to guard the camp, so that it should not be captured.

The blackness was now so thick that nobody could see where to set his foot down. The rain poured, the wind blew, the men were constantly blundering into trees, and falling down, and losing one another, and voices were drowned. To follow a trail was impossible except by crawling and feeling; and every few minutes a halt had to be made, until the stragglers came in.

So that the six miles up-hill seemed sixty, and Robert the Hunter had to confess that he was as blind as all the rest. Even Washington's compass was of no use.

They spent the night searching for the Big Rock. When

in the first gray of the morning they could see, and the Hunter knew where they were, and they found the Rock, they were a sight—muddy and wan, and as wet as muskrats. Seven men had been lost. But Washington had no notion of giving up.

He and John Davidson and Tanacharison and Scarouady talked, while the men shivered and recharged their guns with dry powder. Robert was so tired that he dozed off. But he awakened. Scarouady and Half-King were standing up, to shake hands with Washington.

"We go for a little bloodying of the hatchet, brothers," Scarouady said, with a fierce grin, to the soldiers and the warriors. That was enough to arouse anybody.

The forest had grayed, the storm had lessened to a drizzle again and all the dripping world was shrouded in a cold mist. Half-King led out his Indians, Washington led out his Long Knife Americans; and when they all came to the place in the trail where the two Frenchmen had crossed, Guyasuta and the Buck ran ahead to back-trail again, and this time to find the French camp.

They were not gone long. The French company were hidden down at the foot of Laurel Hill, on the edge of the Great Meadows about one-half mile east of the trail from Gist's! Wah! Yes, they had built bark lodges in a little hollow in the woods, under a ledge of rocks, and were waiting to strike Washington's camp.

"I will summon them to surrender," said Washington to Lieutenant Waggener. "But should they fire upon us I shall not hesitate to answer."

Guyasuta remained to guide the Long Knives by the right; the Mingos filed off by the left; and Robert the Hunter went with the Washington Americans.

The French were astir; for within a short time the heavy air smelled of smoke. The Americans spread out and advanced more cautiously, with guns held so as to shield the locks from the wet. Guyasuta signed that the ledge of rocks was close before. Nothing could be heard from the French camp—the French had thought themselves so well hidden that they needed nobody on watch.

Washington went forward, to peer; and Robert stole after, and the men led by Lieutenant Waggener followed—all without a sound, for the ground was soaked and soft. Somewhere to the left, likewise stealing upon the French, were the Tanacharison party. The French could not escape.

Washington carried no gun, only a stick for a cane. He went around the end of the ledge, as if to call out; then a Frenchman stepped from one of the bark cabins, and saw the soldiers in the woods; he shouted and fired his gun, the French rushed out, and what was said Robert could not hear: both sides were shouting and shooting, and high and terrible rose the Mingo warwhoops.

Several of the French had fallen down; the man who appeared to be their captain was down flat; the French shot from behind their cabins and the Long Knives from behind trees. Washington was standing in the open where the bullets from both sides whizzed; he shouted: "Keep under cover, men! Fire slowly." Now Lieutenant Waggener came running, and he said:

"You are exposed, colonel. Seek cover yourself."

"Not for me, sir," answered Washington. "Go back. I find the situation charming."

In a few minutes he cried out, and waved his stick— "Hold! Cease firing! They ask quarter." Down he rushed, for the French were running here and there, and calling, and the Tanacharison party were into them with the tomahawk, or chasing them through the woods. Scarouady, Aroas, the Buck and the others charged, shrieking the scalp yells, and "bloodying the hatchet."

But Washington hurled them back and ordered them back; and Lieutenant Waggener (who was wounded) and John Davidson and the soldiers interfered; and soon the French were gathered into a bunch.

"Who commands here?" Washington demanded. He was breathless and flushed, and spoke sternly.

The man La Force answered. He it was, and no other; the same cunning, dark man who had made trouble on the trip to Fort Le Boeuf.

"You have killed my commander, the Sieur de Jumonville," said La Force, angrily. "I speak for Monsieur Druillon, next in command. We surrender but you shall pay dearly for this attack upon a peaceful camp."

"I deny your words, sir," Washington replied, turning red. "If you were bent upon peace, why did you hide here in his British Majesty's territory and spy upon us?"

"We came to treat with you and give you summons to withdraw your forces before committing an act of war, as you have done. You refused to listen to the Sieur de Jumonville, who called to you; but you shot him down," accused La Force. "For this you shall pay and pay dearly, sir."

"I will hear no more of such lies," Washington exclaimed. "The act of war was committed when the fort being builded at the Forks in His Majesty's territory was seized by force of arms. You say you would have summoned me. You knew where to find me and could have done so. I would have summoned you, but I had no chance. You opened fire upon me directly you saw me. You will now consider yourselves my prisoners, at the disposal of the Governor of Virginia."

The French had lost Captain de Jumonville and ten men killed, and one man wounded; the prisoners unhurt were twenty-one, and one man had run off. The Long Knife loss was one soldier killed and Lieutenant Waggener and two men wounded.

It was easy to see that Washington was proud of his victory in the first battle that he had ever fought. But the Half-King said:

"Had Washington left matters to us we would have killed them all, for they are spies. But I will send off these few scalps to show the Delaware and Shawnee that the English are in earnest."

This day, which was May 28, 1754, they marched in triumph back to the Great Meadows. Washington gave La Force and Ensign Druillon some of his own clothes; then all the prisoners were sent as a present to the Governor of Virginia.

Half-King at once dispatched a hatchet and a belt of black wampum to King Shingis, bidding him come with his Delawares. Scarouady set out with the scalps and four hatchets and more black wampum, to visit the other Delawares, and the Shawnees, the Wyandots and the Miamis of the Ohio country, and call them to help the English.

If Washington had had more soldiers and enough to eat, things would have been better. But his men numbered only about one hundred, now—without tents and without flour, and with scarcely any meat. And when the French soldier who had escaped barefoot during the battle got to the Forks, the commander there would be hot for revenge.

XIV
Bright Lightning Lends A Hand

Several weeks had passed. On this day, after the middle of the month called June, instead of being with the Washington Long Knives Robert was perched in a tree and watching the great fort named Duquesne, of the French.

This had come about through no other than Bright Lightning, as shall now be told.

Since the battle, matters at Great Meadows had gone only fairly well. Tanacharison had sent to the planting grounds and to Logstown for the Mingo families, and Queen Allaquippa had moved in. But these were the only Delawares, and they, like the Mingos, were mainly women and children, and all had to be fed.

"I will be among the last men to leave the Ohio," Washington had said. While waiting for help he proceeded to build a fort of logs and pickets. That was slow work; the soldiers were thin and weak. Then, before much had been done, another company of Long Knives arrived. Their chief captain was an old soldier named Muse—Major Muse, whom Washington seemed delighted to see. Colonel Fry had died from an accident at Will's Creek, and now Washington was colonel in command of all the Virginia Americans.

Major Muse had brought nine cannon, in wagons, but little food. A Captain James Mackaye was following with a company of soldiers from South Carolina; and Colonel Innes, another old soldier, would come with three hundred and fifty men from North Carolina.

A merry, red-headed young Long Knife doctor named James Craik, whom Washington especially welcomed as a brother, had marched with that other old friend Major Muse, to attend to the sick and wounded. And Andrew Montour the white Seneca, and Trader George Croghan of Pennsylvania, were here. And sometimes Christopher Gist.

Andrew Montour had brought wampum and medals from Assaragoa the Governor, for the Indian chiefs; and one medal for Washington himself. At a council the oldest son of Queen Allaquippa had been given a medal and the English name Colonel Fairfax (who was the odd old man in Virginia). Half-King had been given a medal and the English name Dinwiddie, which was the name of Assaragoa the Governor also, and meant Head of All.

Washington was given the Indian name Connotaucarius or Devourer of Lands. He liked that, but he did not like the pipe that he was obliged to smoke.

Captain Mackaye arrived with his South Carolina company of one hundred men, with sixty cows, but scarcely any ammunition or flour. The South Carolina men would not work on the fort or at cleaning brush unless they were paid extra. They said they were soldiers in the service of the King and not of Virginia; and Captain Mackaye said that they did not have to obey Washington, who commanded only the Virginia Volunteers.

So the Captain Mackaye King's soldiers sat idly, which displeased Tanacharison.

"Washington is too good-natured," he complained. "These men of Mackaye should be made to work or else sent to fight. We stay here from one full moon to another and nothing is done except to start this little thing called a fort, in the open meadow, as if the French would march out of the woods against it and be killed. Meanwhile the French are growing and care nothing about the fort. Why do not the English march on and shut the French up? Where are the other soldiers whom Assaragoa is sending?"

But the Half-King kept scouts out; they brought word that the French at the Forks were growing indeed. Scarouady was still absent with his hatchets and scalps and wampum. The Shingis Delawares had not come in, neither had the Shawnees or Miamis or Wyandots. Scarouady, however, sent the message that certain chiefs would join Washington at Redstone Creek. He asked Washington not to attack the French fort until he should be back.

There now were four hundred men at the Great Meadows. Washington, too, was tired of waiting. No other companies showed up. So he left the Mackaye soldiers to guard the half-completed fort; and he took his three hundred

Long Knives, to cut a road to the mouth of Redstone Creek, at the Monongahela, and build another fort there, nearer to the Forks.

Gist's place, thirteen miles beyond the Laurel Hills, was to be the first stop. And they all had been on the way a week, making only a mile a day in order to open a road through the forest and a rocky gorge, in order that the wagons and the cannon might be hauled; and the war paint of Robert the Hunter had been washed off by sweat and rain; and as tired as the tiredest he was trying to rest, this evening, when he felt a pebble strike his cheek.

He looked aside, and what should he see, in the dusk, but the face of Bright Lightning, White Thunder's daughter, twinkling at him from behind a tree. She beckoned to him to come.

Wah! This was no place for women or girls. The Mingo women and children had stayed down at the Great Meadows, where they would be safe. But Bright Lightning was pretty and spoiled, and usually did as she chose. Thereupon he got up and followed her into the shadows.

"What are you doing here?" he asked. "You'd better go home."

"Listen, Hunter," she said: "Do you want to be a warrior?"

"I am a warrior," he answered. "I do not talk with girls."

"Just because you wear panther claws!" Bright Lightning laughed. "Where is your war paint? I know you did find your way through the dark and you saw scalps taken, but now you cut trees like the white people. You have turned white. All right; be a tree cutter if you like, but I am going to find the French."

"Where?"

"At their great house in the Forks, of course."

"Wah!" exclaimed the Hunter. "You're a girl. Who sent you? What can you do? You're speaking foolish."

"I can count them," declared Bright Lightning.

"That is man's work. Guyasuta and Buck and others are spying," said Robert. "They bring word."

"What word?" Bright Lightning answered scornfully. "One day one thing, one day another. The French are giving presents; they buy the Indians and send out lies to Washington. Even the heart of Tanacharison is getting weak. Yes, I am a girl, but I can go inside the French house, and see, and nobody will mind; then I can come out and tell you. You will tell Washington the truth."

"Wah!" the Hunter exclaimed. "I?"

"Yes." Bright Lightning continued breathlessly. "I have your horse. He will carry us to the Forks. Then you will hide outside and I will go inside, and you shall wait. So if you want to play warrior, come, or I go alone. But two are better than one."

"Good!" said the Hunter. Now he was tired no longer; he was all on fire with the scheme. It was true that many of the Indians who came with word of the French were probably spies, with forked tongues. The French were strong and clever, and gave more presents than the English. But Bright Lightning was smart, too; and women and girls could go in and out of places and not be noticed.

Maybe he should tell Washington first. No! This was Indian work, again. He might not be missed at all; Indians came and went and Washington was busy with the Long Knives, making the road.

So he said only: "Wait." And he ran and got his blanket. He had carried his gun with him from his bed. One did not stir from camp without one's gun.

He joined Bright Lightning. She guided him to the horse, and he mounted and she mounted behind him, and they rode north for the Forks, to learn what the French were doing at their great house named Fort Duquesne.

It was the second morning when they arrived. Over the point of land and over the two rivers that made it, and over the Ohio beyond, there lay a white fog. That was lucky. Out of the fog sounds floated—distant voices of persons and dogs, as if a large village were waking.

"Wah! To go in would be easy for even you," said Bright Lightning. "But you might not get out again. I will go in. When I come out I will meet you here."

So she hurried down into the fog blanket, and left the Hunter here upon the hill above it. The horse had been hidden in a leafy hollow near a spring. Robert promptly climbed into a tree, for the sun was rising and the fog would soon break.

What an amazing sight that was, below, as the fog blanket presently vanished in rifts and tatters! He saw the blue Monongahela and the blue Allegheny and the blue Ohio—all like a forked stick open toward him; and in the fork the strong fort of the French from Onontio, upon the very spot where he had met Washington and Gist bound for Logstown and Venango and Fort Le Boeuf, and from which Lieutenant Ward had been driven.

His hill was an excellent spying spot; from his tree he could look down upon that land, not more than one whoop away. The French had done wonders. They had built a fort shaped like a star; with a high fence of log pickets on the river sides, and a high wall of logs on the other sides, and a wide ditch with the dirt thrown up, surrounding on all the sides. The fence and the walls were pierced for cannon and muskets. Within the fence and walls there were many log houses and many people moving about. The forest had been cut down everywhere within gunshot; upon Robert's side, which was the land side, an enormous cornfield extended from the Monongahela around to the Allegheny; and between the cornfield and the fort ditch a great number of Indians were camped.

Well, Bright Lightning could go through the cornfield and come out among the Indians; and no doubt that was what she was doing. Nobody would care. She was only a girl, and pretty, and the Delawares would be glad to see her.

The point was a busy spot. Robert the Hunter had a view into the fort, where Indians and blue-uniformed soldiers swarmed, and much went on. Indians were constantly coming and going, in canoes or afoot; soldiers were marched out, and were marched in again. Why, Washington had not been told all lies. There were a thousand and more French and Indians here; and what could four hundred half-starved Americans do?

No one bothered him, on his hill. He stayed in the tree most of the day, waiting for Bright Lightning and watching people of the fort. As Bright Lightning did not come back, he knew that she was down there, using her wits while she visited.

This night there was a war-dance by some of the Indians in the camp. The inside of the fort was noisy, too, with lights carried here and there, as though the soldiers were getting ready for a march. Evidently something had been planned.

But in the morning Bright Lightning had not turned up. Inside the fort soldiers had been formed, and Indians in war paint had gathered. That was plain to the Hunter's keen eyes. What was to happen? He wished that he knew. Then, about four hours after sunrise, a great yelling was heard, from up the Allegheny; and the Indians of the fort yelled; and looking, he saw a fleet of canoes and wooden boats, bristling with Indians, dash down from the north. They beached amid a tremendous hooting and cheering; a French officer sprang out, and the Indians followed; they seemed to be more Hurons and French Iroquois; the Delawares and Shawnees and Wyandots greeted them, and the French officer was taken into the fort.

Now what? The soldiers broke ranks, but there was much excitement. The excitement continued all day; late in the afternoon French officers spoke to a great council inside the fort. Their voices reached Robert, but he could not hear what was said. He had begun to be angry with Bright Lightning when she came hurrying through the dusk—

"Quick!" she panted. "Go to Washington, Hunter. Tell him the French march with soldiers and Indians to attack him."

"When?"

"Tomorrow, maybe. That is what they say. I could not come before; now I am glad, because I heard the council. They were getting ready yesterday—five hundred French and a few Miami. The Delaware would not go. You saw those boats. Well, those were all French Indians, sent by Onontio, and that white man named Villiers. Jumonville that Washington and Tanacharison killed was his half-brother. He will lead with his Ottawa and Huron and Iroquois, to take revenge. The French captain chief in the fort spoke hot words in the council. Now the King Shingis and the King Beaver Delaware have accepted the black wampum and the French hatchet, and they are all willing to go to fight the English."

"How many?"

"They are like the corn in the field," said Bright Lightning. "Wah! Do you hurry?"

"Come," exclaimed the Hunter.

"No," replied Bright Lightning. "I am only a girl; you are a warrior and must ride fast. If anybody has followed me, to catch me, that doesn't matter, but no one should catch you. You go to Gist's place quick, on the horse; I am not afraid."

She spoke sense. Robert turned and ran. He knew that Bright Lightning could take care of herself.

XV
In And Out Of Fort Necessity

It was a long way, by day and by night, through the woods and over the hills and across the streams, to Gist's. When he came into sight of the spot he saw that the Washington men had reached it also, and were throwing up a dirt fort.

He rode down upon a lame horse. The Mackaye men were here too, on guard while the Long Knives worked, and Tanacharison had camped near by. Instead of marching on to the mouth of Redstone Creek at the Monongahela in the west, they acted as though they all were getting ready to fight off the French. Maybe they had heard that the French were coming.

So they had, but they had not heard the worst. He found Washington, muddy and hollow-cheeked and stern, wallowing about in the mire, and encouraging his thin, sweat-soaked men. Washington looked at him rather dully—as if maybe he had not missed him; but he said:

"What now? I see the Hunter has been on a journey."

"I come quick from Fort Duquesne to tell of the French," Robert burst out. Tell he did, as fast as he could talk, while several other officers drew near, and Washington's face grew graver.

"Bright Lightning was in the fort?" he asked.

"She counted, and she heard," Robert asserted. "She does not lie. And I saw. The French are more than one thousand. The Indians are half one thousand. The Delaware have taken up the hatchet. They march to catch Washington."

"You have heard, gentlemen," said Washington. "We can believe this boy. The French have received reinforcements again, and I fear are too strong for us in our condition. Peyroney, you will please to summon the officers in council of war to be held immediately in Mr. Gist's house." And he added, to Robert: "I thank the Hunter, and I will thank Bright Lightning. You have done good service."

While the council was being held Robert sat with

Tanacharison. The Half-King was glum.

"Washington is a good man but he gets no help," he complained. "Assaragoa leaves him out in the woods with just a few soldiers and no food. If I could promise presents I could get him plenty of Indians, but he has no presents. He cannot expect the Indians to starve with him and be killed by the French, when Onontio is rich and gives them anything they ask. I will stay and see what happens, but the French are owning the Ohio, with big forts, and the English have nothing. Washington should have moved fast, with many men, and built a great house like I told him to do. But Assaragoa does not listen to my advice. I shall not risk losing my family without any good coming from it. If Washington has sense he will go out from here, which is close to the hills and a very poor place to fight from."

Washington was of the same opinion; for as soon as the council broke up everybody hustled to move away.

They were going back to Great Meadows and to send to Will's Creek for more soldiers and supplies or else march to meet the soldiers and supplies. The wagon horses had given out entirely, with sore feet. So the officers' saddle horses and even Robert's horse were loaded with the ammunition and the scanty camp supplies; Washington left his own baggage, the other officers did the same, when they saw; the soldiers carried what they could upon their backs, and the Long Knife men dragged the nine cannon by hand.

The weather was warm, with heavy thunder storms. Wah, how they all panted and sweat, through the rain and the heat! But in the third day they toiled across the Great Meadows, to the half-finished fort; and this was the first day of July.

The Tanacharison party had beaten the soldiers and were camped with other Mingos, waiting. Then, as the soldiers staggered on to the fort, Washington trudging beside the first file with Robert the Hunter close to him, two figures in breech-clouts and of painted skin strode through the trampled, wet grass to meet them.

One was Scarouady; the other was his son the Buck, a fine young warrior. Scarouady stepped to Washington, and he said, clapping his rifle with his open hand:

"Ho, brother! I am here."

"I am glad to see my brother," Washington answered. "Does he bring news?"

"I bring my son, to fight for Washington," said Scarouady. "We have seen the French upon the war trail, to eat up the English."

"Where?"

"They were yesterday at Redstone Creek. It is well my brother did not go there. They land from canoes paddled up the Monongahela, and march into the woods."

"How many?" Washington asked.

"As many hundreds as the fingers of my hands," said Scarouady. "One-third Indians, two-thirds French. They should be here in two more days. What does my brother plan to do?"

"I will receive them here," replied Washington. "My soldiers are tired and hungry. They cannot travel. If we go on we shall be caught on the road and cut to pieces. Now we will face the French. I see no Indians to help me, but my men are brave."

"You speak well," Scarouady approved. "Chiefs promised to come and help, but they lied. I and my son will help. We have run all the way to find you; now we will run back and watch the French. Let Washington be getting ready with his soldiers and great guns."

Away went the loyal Scarouady and the Buck. Washington trudged on, his gaunt face anxious, to where the men were falling down to rest and eat. Doctor Craik hurried about, giving medicine to those who were sick. Christopher Gist set out for Will's Creek to hasten supplies and the soldier companies that were still there doing nothing, as far as anybody knew.

"Should you communicate with the Governor, tell him we have been without bread for eight days and have no salt with which to preserve our meat," Washington said to Gist. "But if we are provisioned and the French prove no better than they did before, we can hold out."

Washington did not rest. He walked about, with Captain Robert Strobo and Captain Vanbraam the Dutchman (who was stout no longer) and Major Muse, and Captain Mackaye, planning how to complete the fort.

Then the sun sank into the thunder clouds of the west, and night flowed in, and amid the darkness the tired guards walked their beats where, any moment, an Indian might spring with the hatchet.

Nothing happened this night. Early in the morning all the Long Knife Americans who could stand were set at work digging ditches and chopping trees and hauling logs, while the Mackaye soldiers kept guard. Washington himself, Vanbraam, Muse and other officers seized axes and helped; and young Captain Robert Strobo (a slender, lively, handsome man with round brown face and bright dark eyes) showed where the ditches and the walls should be put.

The old ditch with dirt thrown up was changed until it formed a triangle about thirty paces on a side, and the logs were laid on top of the dirt. On two of the sides another ditch was dug, a little way in front. The place was the best possible, on a piece of level ground two hundred and fifty paces wide, between hills, with a creek running through, for water— although there was to be water in plenty without it, they were to find out.

The nearest trees where an enemy could hide were on a point sixty paces distant, and these trees were being cut as fast as possible and used for logs.

This digging, chopping, hauling and piling was hard work for worn-out men. The Tanacharison people did not seem to think much of the fort, which Half-King called a "little thing," not large enough to stay in—saying that Washington was foolish to expect the French to march down to it and be killed.

However, what better could be done, now? By sunset the outer ditch was only knee-deep, and the dirt of the entrenchment had been raised by only one or two logs. Then in the dusk Scarouady's son came running. The French, in great number, were at Gist's place, looking for Washington. They had fired upon Gist's place before they had learned that nobody was there. Scarouady had stayed to watch them.

All this night it rained—and a miserable night that was. Early in the morning the men got up, and in the rain ate what could be eaten; guards were posted far out to give warning should the French be near; and Washington and Captain Strobo decided that more trees upon the wooded point should be cut down. Most of the Tanacharison people were leaving into the woods where the women and children would be safer than in the fort which had no roof and was too small.

The tree chopping went on slowly. Then, in the rain, who should come, from the other end of the meadow, but Bright Lightning! Yes, it was she, and by the way she hurried she was very tired. Robert seemed to be the one who saw her first—a weary little figure. He ran to meet her.

"Ho, Hunter!" she gasped. "Tell Washington the French are less than four miles off. Nine times one hundred, with many Indians in front. They come."

And Bright Lightning sank down. Her feet were bare and bleeding; her deer-skin dress was torn. She had been a long time out.

Robert made haste to tell Washington that the French were on this side of the Laurel Hills. He had not got to where Washington was helping chop the trees, when he heard a gunshot in the forest in that direction. Next a soldier staggered down the slope there.

"Injuns!" he shouted. "The enemy!"

He was one of the out-post sentinels; an Indian had fired upon him and wounded him.

All the sentries were running in now. The tree chopping ceased; the officers began to form their companies at the fort. And next another figure appeared bounding down into the meadow—and Robert heard the scalp halloo of Scarouady.

Here came Scarouady, with a dripping scalp in one hand and his rifle in the other. Huzzah! He had avenged the wounded soldier. And he cried, panting in:

"The French soldiers one short mile; the woods are full of Ottawa and Huron. I have struck the Ottawa. Make ready, Long Knives."

Although the Mingos of Tanacharison had proved weak, and the Delawares and the Shawnees were not helping, it was good to have Scarouady and his son and the brave little Bright Lightning faithful.

Pretty soon figures of both Indians and French soldiers could be seen moving among the trees of a hill in the northwest a quarter of a mile away; and on a sudden a great smoke gushed and a tremendous volley rolled across the meadow. But never a ball dropped anywhere near.

The Long Knives and the Mackaye company stood in line in the open meadow in front of the ditches, with Washington walking up and down before them. The blue flag of Virginia drooped over the centre of the Washington men, and the red flag of the King drooped over the centre of the fort.

"Do not answer," Washington ordered. "They cannot harm us from that distance. They only seek to draw us from our position. Wait them here, and when they descend, fire at close quarters. They cannot stand against our balls well delivered."

But the French did not come out of the woods. They fired another volley or two, their Indians screeched; and seeing that Washington stood firm, waiting them, they began to march about. A stirring sight they made, from the glimpses of them: part of them in regular uniform, and part in rangers' hunting shirts, and the Indians scuttling painted for war.

By this day the men of Washington who were able to fight had shrunk to about three hundred and fifty, including the Mackaye company.

It wasn't long before shots commenced to pepper from the point where trees had been left, and from another slope a little farther. That was killing range.

"The rascals will not show themselves," said Washington, to Major Muse. "Do you ask Captain Mackaye to station his men within the log trenches, and my rangers will hold the outside ditches. Then if that tempts those fellows to assault, let them come."

This was quickly done. The Captain Mackaye King's soldiers knelt behind the log-capped breastworks, ready to serve their muskets and the cannon; and the Long Knife soldiers knelt in the ditches in front.

The French and Indian fire increased, so that the balls whistled thickly. The French soldiers were covered by the trees of the point and the slope sixty yards and one hundred yards away; the Indians climbed into the trees themselves; and from above the fort they all could shoot down into it.

Then the Virginians and the Mackaye men began to answer with muskets and cannon, so that the ground and the air shook, and one could scarcely see through the smoke.

The battle lasted all the rest of the day. The cows ran hither and thither, and the French Indians shot them. In the ditches and in the fort itself men were being struck. Ensign Peyroney was badly wounded. The cannon had been placed upon dirt platforms to shoot over the logs, but the gunners were picked off when they reloaded and aimed. The dirt of the breastworks got soft from the rain, and flowed down into the trenches. Much of this the Hunter learned a little later, for now he was out in the ditches with the Long Knives, who shot well. Every little while an Indian fell from a tree, or a French soldier sprang up and toppled down.

But the weather fought against Washington. He sought no cover—he moved along, behind his men, encouraging them, and so did Doctor Craik, seeking the wounded. In the afternoon another thunder storm broke; the rain poured in sheets, the men could not fire their muskets, and the ditch was almost level with water.

Washington gave orders and they all went back to crowd into the trenches of the fort, which were not much better. After the thunder storm the sky cleared somewhat. The fight opened again. The Washington men could not get out, the French dared not come in.

"If we can hold till morning, I think we have them whipped," said Washington to Major Muse.

"That, if our ammunition holds out also," said Major Muse. "The men have scarce a handful of bullets and a dozen charges of powder apiece; the guns are fouled and no way of cleaning them."

"The French may be in worse shape, sir," Washington declared.

Now it was getting too dark to shoot. The little fort was littered with dead and wounded; one-third of all the Long Knives and the Mackaye soldiers were out of action. But, as Washington had said, the French might be no better off.

Then from the dusk on the edge of the nearest woods somebody called in French:

"Hallo, Messieurs the English!"

"Hallo!" shouted Washington.

"I would come in. We offer a parley to save the English further loss of life."

Vanbraam translated.

"Tell him to keep away," Washington directed. "We wish no parley. Besides," he added, "the French are weakening and to let them see our condition would encourage them."

So Vanbraam told the man to keep away. Then pretty soon the man called again. He asked that an officer be sent out to talk. Washington consented to this. Ensign Peyroney spoke good French, but he was too sorely wounded to move. Accordingly Captain Jacob Vanbraam went out to the French and the Indians.

He was gone a long time. When at last he came back he brought a paper that made terms. He read the paper by light of a candle to Washington, and Washington shook his head.

"We will never agree to terms so dishonorable," he said. "The only thing to which I will consent is the privilege of marching out with all our forces and property, and of retiring unmolested. Captain de Villiers may then have the fort, such as it is."

Captain Jacob Vanbraam made several trips back and forth, in the dark; and each time the paper was changed by the French captain, and was reread by Vanbraam by the light of the flickering candle held under a cloak spread over it.

Then while Robert was squatting among the weary men who waited anxiously Scarouady's son, the Buck, touched him on the shoulder.

So Robert rose, and followed the Buck out of the fort, and around to where Half-King was camped at a little distance, on high ground among some trees.

Scarouady and Aroas and Fairfax, the son of Queen Allaquippa, were here sitting beside Half-King who was lying down wrapped in a blanket.

"You have been listening to the talk between Washington and the French captain," said Tanacharison. "What is going on down there? Do the English surrender?"

"Washington says the French will have to let him march away or he will fight," the Hunter answered.

"Wah!" grumbled Tanacharison. "That is right. The

French have had enough. They are cowards and hide in the woods, but the English are fools and do nothing at all. I lent you to Washington to learn the white ways. Now it seems to me the Indian ways are better. The Mingos are going to Aukwick to live till the French and English are done fighting. I wish you to come with me."

But Aukwick, which in the Mohawk tongue was Oquaga or Place of Wild Grapes, was an old Iroquois town far away, upon the Susquehanna River in New York; and Robert's heart sank.

"I am Washington's man," he said. "I cannot leave Washington."

"You are not his son; you are mine," replied Tanacharison. "Now the French have bewitched me for having killed the Jumonville men and I am sick. I will go where the French cannot reach me. You will be of no use to Washington, for the French have driven him out. I need you more than he does. Those are my words."

Half-King did indeed appear sick. After staying for a time the Hunter went back, down to the fort. It was midnight, and Washington and Captain Mackaye were just signing the French paper.

Evidently they had got good terms. The French did not know, but there were thirty dead and seventy wounded, and little powder and ball, and less than two days' food.

The dead had to be buried and the wounded cared for. Just how to tell Washington that Tanacharison had taken him away Robert could not figure; but of course tell Washington he should. And finally he found a chance.

Washington, who was tired out and looked sad, nodded gravely.

"You must go with the Half-King," he said. "He is sick and needs you. I do not need you. Tell him I call him brother and he must not fight against the English, for the French cannot keep this country."

"When you come again I will help you, Washington," said the Hunter. "I am American."

Scarouady had returned. He stepped forward; and he said:

"Half-King old and sick, Connotaucarius. No fight um

French, no fight um English. Me, Scarouady, brudder to English, fight um French. Me watch um. Next time you come, send for Scarouady."

Then he shook hands with Washington and patted him on the back. The Hunter followed him and the Buck, to sleep upon the hill.

Early in the morning they all were up, to see what was going to happen. The fort had been busy much of the night by the light of fires; and it was still busy with men getting ready to march away. Some of the French were there waiting. Pretty soon the Washington soldiers, and the Mackaye soldiers started carrying a flag and beating their drums. Upon their backs or in litters of blankets they bore wounded men while other wounded men hobbled after. But they moved bravely, without fear of the French and Indians looking on.

It was a long file. Before it all had left the fort Tanacharison said:

"I have seen enough. Washington is not a man to give up easily, but now the French are here. Let us go too, or they will make me so I cannot travel."

They set out. The Half-King was in pain from his sickness, but when by a roundabout way they reached Gist's place, in the afternoon, he felt better and they stopped again to rest. Gist's was deserted. After they had rested for a time the Buck came in from his look-out on the trail.

"What is it?" Tanacharison asked.

"The French are coming. They will be here soon," the Buck reported.

Tanacharison groaned.

"I feel sick. If I stay I shall die or else lose my mind to the French. We will put distance between us and them, and get out of their evil power."

The Buck and Robert had followed only a little way when in the woods the Buck spoke into Robert's ear.

"Wah! We will not run off. We are warriors. Let us turn back and see what these French are going to do."

The Buck was a fine young man, not much older than Robert. No one could ask for a better partner. His words sounded good. Therefore the Hunter dropped back with him; and they two lay in the brush where they could watch the

French come into Gist's.

Presently the column descended from the road through the woods into the flat where Gist's houses were and where Washington had made his ditches. Ottawa and Huron scouts led, walking swiftly; then came the French commanders, and the soldiers and Canadian rangers, and more Indians: all merry, and many loaded with plunder from the Great Meadows.

But see! Who were those? Amid the blue and white uniforms of the French there was a flash of red: the English color!

"Wah!" uttered the Buck. "They have prisoners."

Robert's heart sank again. One of the prisoners was tall. The French had kept Washington! Washington would be a great prize. Those were either Long Knife officers, or else Mackaye men, for the Long Knife soldiers themselves had been poorly dressed in all kinds of clothes.

The French marched down to Gist's; the Indians ran about, among the houses; the soldiers helped, and soon the buildings were burning and the ditch was being filled up. The two men with red coats and trousers sat apart, with French officers.

"They are being saved for torture," said the Buck. "The Ottawa will eat them, to be made brave with their flesh."

"No!" Robert cried. "One of them looks like Washington. I am going in."

"What good will that do?"

"I will find out who they are. They will know me. You will run and tell Scarouady to come and help."

"Ho!" Buck answered. "That will do no good either. They are being taken to the French big house first, as a show, and will be well watched. Nobody from the outside can help them."

"I will go in and let them see me," said the Hunter. "Then they will know that help is coming. I am American."

"You can do no good, and the French will keep you and send you to Onontio; or else the Huron will eat you."

"I go," repeated the Hunter. "You can wait here and see what happens, and then you can tell Scarouady."

The Buck laughed.

"Wah! You are a boy but you are brave. You speak my own mind. We will go in together. We are Mingo, and the French try to make friends of the Mingo. They and the Ottawa and Huron will pretend to be glad to see us. Let us wipe off our paint. Come, and we shall fool them."

The Buck stood up, and with Robert at his heels went right down for the enemy camp.

XVI
In And Out Of Fort Duquesne

Huzzah! Neither of the two red-coated men was Washington. The tall one who might have been Washington was the young Long Knife captain named Strobo, who had planned Fort Necessity. And the other, short and square, was Captain Jacob Vanbraam of Dutch Land.

They were not tied, but this counted nothing, because they could not run away. Captain Vanbraam seemed to be sputtering in his funny French with the French officers, while the handsome Captain Strobo sat silently, sending his brown eyes roving about. And whether he saw Robert, Robert did not know; but of course it would not do to take any notice of him or Vanbraam.

So they two went straight in, with the Hunter's heart beating a little swiftly at the sight of the sleek Ottawas and bristle-headed Hurons, of the French north, painted for war. First a sharp-eyed Ottawa gave an alarm call, then a French sentry shouted; and soldiers sprang to arms and the Ottawas and Hurons raced with their guns.

But when they all saw only two boys, they waited in silence, until the Ottawas and Hurons cried:

"Mingo!"

Then Ottawas and Hurons met them, and grabbed them and jostled them, seized their guns and, threatening them with the hatchet, marched them to the French captains.

The French captain who was chief called:

"Enough, my children! These are friends."

Thereupon the Ottawas and Hurons stood aside, while the captain smilingly questioned by the mouth of a darker, wiry man who spoke in the Iroquois and wore gay buckskin beaded with the Ottawa chief-sign.

"My young brothers are from our friends the Mingo?"

"I am Oneida; he Seneca," replied the Buck. "Mingo."

"The children of Onontio welcome the Mingo. My young brothers have come on a visit?"

"We wish to see the French and rest at their fire," said

the Buck.

"That is good. My young brothers are alone?"

"Yes. We are hunting, and are tired and hungry," said the Buck.

"Very good. My young brothers shall rest and eat. By what name shall we know our brothers?"

"I am Deer-With-Horns, he is Panther-Killer," said the Buck.

The captain chief smiled and gave smooth words.

"Let Deer-With-Horns and Panther-Killer rest and eat with their brothers of Onontio who owns this country. When they wish to leave they will go to tell the Mingo that the French father is generous and strong. He invites all the Mingo to come in to the big house at Dekanawida and receive presents. For now the English have been driven away forever. Your brothers from the north will tell you so."

With that, the Ottawas and Hurons who had been listening were about to step forward and bid to a feast, and the Buck and the Hunter might have moved about freely, and everything would have gone off well, had not Jacob Vanbraam suddenly sprang up and hailed Robert with stupid greeting.

"It is the Hoonter! Yah! Now I know him. Goot boy. Maybe you been from Washington, eh? You coom to see how we get along, eh?" And he grasped the Hunter's hand and shook it.

"Wah!" grunted the Buck, turning away quickly. "He is drunk."

That was so, but made no difference. All had heard; and whether the words were understood or not, all had seen, too, and knew that the man in the red coat and the Hunter had been together before.

The French officers exchanged glances. Captain Strobo sat flushing as if vexed. Vanbraam gabbled in broken French and English, and patted the Hunter's shoulder and called him "goot boy," and Strobo called sharply to him.

The French laughed. The captain chief and another captain who was the same Mercier that had summoned Ensign Ward to surrender talked together rapidly; then the interpreter mingled with the Ottawa and Huron, passing word to them.

"Go with your brothers of Onontio," said the French captain, now. "Sit by their fires and eat."

This time he spoke in French; for the tipsy Jacob Vanbraam was babbling in spite of the angry Strobo:

"He iss a goot boy. He iss a smart boy. He speak English and a leetle French, and why not should I talk with him. Mebbe he coom from Washington. I am no prisoner. We but stay a leetle while and den we go home. Yah! He shall tell Washington we all right."

That had finished things for the Buck and Robert. They were taken away by the French Indians, to a fire, and given food; but while they ate they knew that they were under suspicion.

The interpreter came and sat with them; and a haughty, piercing-eyed Ottawa chief, plainly a great warrior, but not of councillor age yet, put shrewd questions to them.

"My young warrior brothers are from the English?"

"No," said the Buck. "We have heard the French are strong and wish to see them."

"My young brothers have been in war paint," said the Ottawa chief. Yes, his eyes were quick eyes. "Do they wear war paint for the French or for the English?"

Ho! This was a poser.

"The Ottawa chief does not know the Mingo war paint," the Buck retorted. "When Oneida and Seneca put on the war paint the Ottawa stay home."

"Ho!" the chief exclaimed. "You speak to Pontiac. Those are the foolish words of a boy."

Pontiac! He was a great war chief of the Ottawa and he was angered. But the dark man in Ottawa dress interrupted.

"They are brave boys; we can see they are warriors. There is no war between the Mingo and the Ottawa. All are brothers under the flag of Onontio."

"Langlade knows that the Mingo helped the English kill the brother of Villiers," said Pontiac. "They have French scalps. The Mingo are dogs that bite the hand that feeds. The red-coat fat man says these boys come from the English. The Mingo send in their boys as spies."

And another Ottawa who had been eying the Hunter

cried:

"This boy was at Venango with the Englishman Washington. He is the son of Tanacharison. He will take word of us to Tanacharison and Washington. He is a spy."

Then Ottawas and Hurons began to jeer and threaten, and their words were not pleasant.

"Give them to us, Langlade," they begged. "Let them go back without eyes and tongues, and tell what they have seen."

Langlade held up his hand. His was a famous name, too; for he was half Ottawa, and was a French Ranger captain, and had led the Indians who had wiped out Pickawillanie of the Miamis and had eaten old Chief Britain.

"Wait, brothers!" he bade. "Would you harm boys who come in boldly? What have we to fear?" And he smiled upon Robert. "Tell me why you came and you shall be safe," he said. "I am Captain Langlade. Who sent you?"

"Nobody sent us. We saw you from the woods and we came down," answered the Hunter.

"Is Tanacharison your father?"

"Feather Eagle, Delaware, my father; my mother the White Woman," answered the Hunter. "I live with Tanacharison, but I am American."

"Where is Tanacharison, that he does not come in too, to his friends from Onontio?"

"Tanacharison is sick. He goes to Aukwick."

"You know that red-coat captain, who spoke to you?"

"Yes. I went with the red-coat captain to hunt for him and Washington on the trail to Venango two winters ago."

"I can see you are a brave boy and speak the truth," said Langlade, smoothly. "You will be a warrior." And he asked of the Buck:

"You are Oneida. You have a father?"

"Wah!" the Buck uttered proudly. "I tell no lies. My father is a great chief of the Oneida Mingo. He is Scarouady. The Ottawa and Huron have heard of him."

"Scarouady!" The word was repeated. Yes, the French Indians had heard of Scarouady.

"It is well," said Langlade. "We do not wish to war with Tanacharison and Scarouady. The French father has sent for them, and we wait for them to come. If they have listened to lies and have thought of taking up the hatchet for the English, that shall be forgotten. Onontio is generous, and loves the Mingo like he loves the Delaware, the Shawnee, the Ottawa and the Huron. All are his children. Now you shall stay and see what manner of men the men of Onontio are. Then when you go back safe, the Seneca and the Oneida will know."

"When we go back safe," remarked the Buck, a little later, to the Hunter. "Wah! That may not be for a long time."

That sounded like sense. Following Langlade's pleasant speech, as if they had received orders the Ottawas and the Hurons were very friendly indeed. They offered food, and dry moccasins, and even the haughty Pontiac wheedled the two "young warriors from our brothers." Now all the talk was of the strong French and of the weak English, and of the love of Onontio for the Senecas and Oneidas, and of the presents to be had at Fort Duquesne, and of the French traders who were so much more generous than the English traders, and of the foolishness of depending upon the English anyway. The English had been driven out forever; the white flag of the King of France was greater than that red flag of the English King; all the Ohio Country belonged to the French and to their brothers the Indians.

"Our two young brothers shall come with us to the French fort and see, so that they may understand," the Ottawas and Hurons prated.

"We thank the Ottawa and Huron, but the fort at Dekanawida is far and we must go to Aukwick," the Buck answered. "We have seen the strength of Onontio and will go in the morning and tell the Mingo chiefs at Aukwick."

"No," smiled Pontiac. "You shall be guests in the lodge of Pontiac until your eyes are open and there are no English in them. Those two red-coats are the last of the English; soon they will be gone too."

"Wah!" uttered the Buck. "The Ottawa will dance their scalps at Dekanawida?"

"The Ottawa will dance as many scalps as there are English, if the English come again," laughed Pontiac. "But these two dogs are kept by the French until all the French that have been stolen by the Englishman Washington are sent back. This does not concern my young brothers," Pontiac added, with a crafty look. "With the English they would be wet and hungry; but with the French they are dry and well fed. They have nothing to do with the English. The French have switched the English home like squaws; and Tanacharison and Scarouady will refuse to listen more to the false song of the little English bird in the woods."

So the Ottawas and the Hurons cunningly bragged, flattered and pretended friendship, and promised great things at Fort Duquesne; and the Hunter noticed that his gun and the Buck's were not given back, and that he was not permitted to move out of reach, or to get near Vanbraam or Captain Strobo; and it was plain that he and the Buck were in a trap. To the French fort they must go; and there, what?

"We shall be as wise as the bear," said the Buck, at his first chance. "They will not harm us. They fill us with lies; and then they will tell the Mingo to come and get us. Let us pretend, too, and learn all we can. Already some of the Mingo are weak. Guyasuta has listened, and Joncaire has sent words and presents to Scarouady."

"Scarouady will go to the French?" stammered the Hunter.

"No! He is true to Washington. But let us pretend and learn all we can, so that when we escape we shall have news to take."

They each slept this night between two Ottawas. In the morning the French marched on, to the Monongahela at Redstone Creek. Here they burnt and pulled down the storehouse and cabins of the Ohio Company. Canoes had been waiting; and they and the Ottawas and Hurons got in and down the Monongahela they all went, to Fort Duquesne.

What a tremendous welcome they got! The Ottawas and Hurons and many of the French Rangers fired their muskets in token of victory; the guns of the fort answered, the Indians there rushed for the bank, shooting and yelling; the canoes responded again, the men piled out, and were escorted by a mob into the clearing around the fort.

All the time up to now neither Robert nor the Buck had had a chance to speak with Captain Strobo or Vanbraam; but in the midst of the jostling and confusion the Hunter heard a voice in his ear.

"Quick! Did Washington send you?" hissed Captain Strobo.

"No. We came to help."

"Good! Wait. See me later in fort. Be careful."

Then they were separated. Strobo and Vanbraam were taken on into the fort; the Buck and Robert were lodged outside, where the Indians celebrated.

Whether they two could have slipped away, no one might say. The Buck was for trying, this very night; but when Robert told him of Strobo, he said:

"Wah! We will wait. I am your brother; we two are one."

They knew that they were watched to see if they would try to escape. And they were well treated, for the French very much wished to win the Mingos over. A few Mingos were here, from up-river; a few Delawares from the west; but the main horde were Ottawas, Hurons, Potawatomis, and Ojibwas from the far north. The other Delawares and Shawnees were waiting to see what the English would do now.

After a couple of weeks the watchfulness lessened. Scouts reported that no English were coming. The fort gates stayed open. The Buck and the Hunter were even permitted to wander in and look about. Vanbraam and Captain Strobo appeared to be well treated also. They were not under guard; they walked and sat with the French officers; it was true that they were being held only until the Governor of Virginia sent back the prisoners taken by Washington when Jumonville was killed.

Vanbraam drank freely—a jolly man, he, and foolish. But Strobo was smart. He pretended to be happy, and yet his eyes were always darting about, and his mind was busy. Then, one morning as he passed Robert he said, without pausing:

"Meet me behind storehouse at sunset. Tell nobody."

Something was to happen! "Tell nobody," Captain Strobo had said; by that, Robert was not to tell even the Buck. There were many eyes and ears in this Fort Duquesne.

So at sunset he was behind the fort storehouse—in back of it where it stood near the pickets of the east side along the Monongahela River. And here, to his astonishment, the Buck was crouching; and around the corner of the house here came

Captain Strobo, walking rapidly.

The place already was dim with shadow. Captain Strobo spoke to Robert and the Buck.

"Here are letters. One of you go to John Croghan in Pennsylvania, one to Washington. Will you?"

The Buck caught at the words.

"Wah! I find Croghan. Quick!"

"Good. The Hunter to Washington," smiled Strobo. "One of you will get through. If these papers are captured, I die. If you lose them, tell what you have seen; all about the fort and the people. The Indians are not scouting; the French are careless. Let the English strike. They must not wait till we are safe out. They must keep La Force. He is dangerous. Our lives are nothing. We are not to be thought of. I would gladly die if the fort might be taken. You understand?"

Robert nodded. The Buck did not understand all, but he understood a part.

"We hear a chief," he said in Iroquois.

He stuffed his letter inside his belt; Robert did the same.

"Each for himself, Hunter," said the Buck. "I will see you at Aukwick."

Captain Strobo had turned away, to be gone before anybody should interfere.

"Now!" prompted the Buck. "It is time."

He put his moccasins in his belt and clinging with his toes and fingers to the logs set on end twelve feet high and forming the stockade he shinned right up. Robert was after. They vaulted over, landing lightly; but they had no more than straightened after tying on their moccasins again ere a tall figure rose right before them.

"My young brothers are going to hunt owls?" asked Pontiac. "Or do they wish to see their fathers?"

He reached for the Buck. The Buck might have drawn hatchet or knife and struck to kill; but Robert doubled up and drove forward right into Pontiac's stomach. Pontiac doubled up, too; and his breath gushed in a loud whoop. As the two messengers raced on they heard another whoop, a real alarm whoop, from Pontiac's lips. He could not run yet, but he could yell.

The stockade was skirted by a ditch with dirt

breastworks. They scampered along the stockade and were almost at the next corner. But people were running about inside the fort; there were shouts and thud of moccasins from around the corner, and a sentry's musket flamed—Bang!— from the bastion there, calling for the guard.

They swerved sharply, and scrambled through the shallow ditch and fairly bounded over the breastworks seven feet high and were outside, between the breastworks and the Monongahela.

It was lucky that on the river side of the Forks the French had few guards. Now the Hunter and the Buck made for the water.

"I go down, you go up," the Buck panted. He dived from the bank, into the Monongahela; Robert dived. And that was the last he saw of the Buck for some time.

The Buck could swim swiftly down with the current. No doubt he planned to enter the Allegheny and land and cut through the woods for the east where George Croghan lived. But to swim up the Monongahela was a different proposition for the Hunter. Besides, here came the Ottawas and Hurons pell-mell, to their canoes. They, of course, would think that the two boys were swimming across. The river was dark, the Hunter sank low, paddling just enough to keep afloat. The current tugged at him; he never could escape those canoes now spreading from the landing place above him. He turned back. Aha! His groping hands felt a snag—the roots of an old grounded tree, in an eddy of a curve of the high bank. He dragged himself forward, sinking still lower underneath the jagged roots and throwing his head back until only his nose was above for air.

On swept the canoes, bearing warriors to beat the river and to search the shore beyond. For a long time he waited, until the hue and cry had died. Then he left the roots, and was paddling out when he sank low again.

Here came another canoe, and it paused almost over him. It held two Indians.

"They are Mingos, and like eels," said one. "It would be like them to hide along the bank until we passed."

"You talk sense," said the other. "Let us try along the bank up river; they are not down river."

They dug with their paddles—one in the bows, one in the stern. The Hunter gently extended his hand; it closed upon the stem of the canoe, and kicking under water and gently stroking he went with the canoe. Pretty soon one of the Indians spoke again.

"The canoe is heavy."

"Wah! It is the current. You are weak in your arms, brother," answered the other. "Dig deeply."

At this, Robert almost laughed.

With the two paddlers interested in searching the banks and the dim surface, the canoe towed him quite a distance up stream. Then it stopped, above the landing place, and the Indians whooped. Whoops replied to them. They were no-news whoops. The other canoes were coming back.

"They have found nothing," said one Indian. "The two young rascals are hiding. Let us go home and wait till daylight."

Robert drew breath and sank, swimming under water. When he broke out again the canoe had gone; and he veered for the shore and landed at last, and scuttling through the shallows he climbed out, well up stream. He rounded a cornfield and was in the woods. Whether he could yet get away he did not know; but they had not caught the Buck.

The night had settled; all the woods were black. After stumbling for a mile or two he also had to stop, and wait for daylight.

Now he was south of the fort, upon the fort side of the Monongahela. The Ottawas and Hurons would surely scout both sides of the river, in the morning, to find the trail of him and the Buck. He must be up at dawn, and making onward for Will's Creek once more, to seek Washington. Before he curled to nap in a bed of leaves he clapped his hand to his belt. The letter from Strobo to Washington was gone!

Ho! He had lost it! It had slipped out, probably while he was running and stumbling from the river. Now what to do? He could go on and tell Washington about Strobo and about the fort—but if that letter were found upon his trail and taken back to the French, then Captain Strobo would die as a spy.

This should not be. He could see nothing now in the woods; his back trail was buried in the darkness: but he must hasten, the first thing, by morn light, and find that letter himself before the enemy pounced upon it. Of course, he would be heading right into the scouting parties——

Well, he had to make the try. He might at least find the letter and hide it before he was caught.

The Hunter slept uneasily this night. He was up early in the awakening day, and back-trailing; hungry he was, too. The forest was still dim, he could not travel fast as yet, for the little trail he had left was faint; and with his eyes upon the ground he had gone not half way to the river when he heard sudden distant whoops.

Those whoops he knew. They were rallying whoops— the enemy had discovered his foot-prints where he had left the river! Wah! Ottawas and Hurons would be coming fast. He was liable to run into them—he hoped that the letter had been lost in the river—about himself he did not care, and he was determined to go as far as he could, in order to save Captain Strobo if possible. And meanwhile the Buck would be getting away.

He trotted, searching for the glimmer of the letter. The woods were beginning to echo. If he could find that letter, and hide it—huzzah! He had it, he had it! And he picked it up and he turned with a bound, and to a burst of view-halloo from the leading scouts he bolted full speed. Perhaps he could get off, after all.

He went leaping, straining, scudding like a hare, with the shouts in gleeful pursuit. So once again he was fleeing, as he had fled the Cherokee; but it took better legs now to catch Robert the Hunter—fifteen years old, hard and lean and bred to the woods the same as an Indian.

Up slope and down slope and through the levels he plunged; and the shouts seemed to string out behind him. He doubled and side-stepped, and broke his trail, and by this gained time; and he ever had his eyes alert for a tree or a rock ledge where he might cover up long enough to throw the enemy off the scent.

His legs were getting heavy, and his breath was short. From another slope he looked back upon his trail. Ugh! Two Ottawas were closing in upon him—they were plain in sight of him, and he was plain in sight of them. They had appeared suddenly, they shouted and he glanced aside and he saw another Indian (a Huron) burst from cover on his right as by a short cut, to head him off.

The Ottawas were not shooting, but the Huron dashed on with hatchet lifted. And Robert swerved a little and in last spurt legged again. He could not throw the letter away here, before the eyes of Ottawas and Hurons. Now all he hoped for was to win the top of the slope, and dive over and get rid of the letter there. Then they could capture him and do what they pleased with him.

The Huron whooped shrilly. The slope rang to the cries of him and the Ottawas. The cries ceased; the pursuit was saving breath—glancing behind again Robert saw the Huron bearing in, his painted face a-scowl, his skin sweaty, his hatchet raised. The top of the slope loomed with thick brush into which a boy might dive. Run, Hunter! Now! He almost could feel the Huron's clutch, he could see only dimly—he lunged to the top, and he made another leap, and a great blow upon the head sent him spinning; and to cheers and crack of guns he sank into blackness.

XVII
Scouting For The Grenadiers

It seemed to Robert, while he lay panting and kicking and trying to wake, that a battle had been raging over him. He knew that he was wet with cold water, and that fingers were busy upon his head; and at last he looked into a face black-whiskered, black-eyed, a face very dark and stern, but ready to smile: the face, yes, of the Black Rifle!

Robert struggled to sit up in a jiffy. The Black Rifle was a fearsome man—an Indian-killer. And around-about there were other white-men, in buckskin and long hair, powder flasks and bullet pouches, hatchets and knives—several of them with fresh scalps at their belts.

He groped for his letter. It was gone again! The Black Rifle laughed silently.

"You miss something?" he asked in Delaware.

"You have it?" the Hunter stammered in English. His head hurt him. He put up his hand; his head was bandaged and wet; his hand came away red.

Captain Jack the Black Rifle continued to laugh inside himself.

"Hah, boy! You have a hard skull. The Huron hatchet glanced like a chip. Where were you going?"

"I carry letter to Washington. You got it?"

"No."

What! It was lost? Had the Ottawas found it after all? The agony of the Hunter's head was nothing compared with the agony of his heart. He would have tottered to his feet, but the hand of the Black Rifle pressed him down.

"Lie still. The letter's on its way."

"To Washington?"

"Aye, or to the Governor of Virginia. That's what the address said on the inside." They had acted quickly, these Black Rifle men! "We thought you dead. Who sent you?"

"No tell," replied the Hunter.

"Very good. Then you needn't. You've been in the river; those French Injuns didn't chase you for nothing; aye, you're a brave boy. You shall have that Huron's gun and fixin's. And there'll be scalps missing at Fort Duquesne." Captain Jack laughed shortly. "Now, lads! We must put more distance behind us ere the pack howls on our trail."

A very giant of a man picked Robert up; they all filed rapidly into the woods.

The Black Rifle's band had been scouting upon Fort Duquesne. Now they were returning into Pennsylvania with the news that they had. The Hunter had a gun again, but a boy with his scalp ripped open by a tomahawk and with his head throbbing could not go to Will's Creek alone. Every mile in company with the Captain Jack men took him farther from Will's Creek and nearer to Aukwick, and Tanacharison and Scarouady and (he hoped) the Buck.

Therefore to Aukwick he went, instead of to Will's Creek.

The Buck had got through! Here he was, his own message delivered. Strobo would be glad when he knew.

Tanacharison was sick in bed. All this fall the Mingos at Aukwick waited for word that the English were to drive the French from the Ohio. Scarouady made a trip to Onondago, to speak for the English before the council of the Iroquois. The Iroquois were growing tired. Said old Chief Hendrick, the Mohawk, to the English in Albany:

"The English pay us no attention, but the French are wise and active, and are always inviting us. You accuse the French of many things. When the French come, you run away. Look about your country. You have no forts. The French can come and turn you out of doors. They are men; they are making forts everywhere. But you are bare and open."

More and more Iroquois were going over to the French. Captain Joncaire had persuaded the Delawares and the Shawnees. The Mingos at Aukwick listened to George Croghan but many outside travelled to Fort Duquesne where the French gave presents.

Washington had gone home from Will's Creek. Maybe he had grown tired, too, of waiting for help. The Governor of Virginia had not given the French back the prisoners taken by Washington; and it was said that Strobo and Vanbraam had been sent to Canada by the French, as prisoners. But the package carried by the Buck to George Croghan had contained a map of Fort Duquesne; this also had gone to the Governor of Virginia, and why Assaragoa did not act, nobody knew.

Old Tanacharison died this fall. No doubt the French had made him sick, because he had fought them. Scarouady was appointed Half-King. That was good. He was not afraid of the French. And the winter wore on, and it was rumored that the King across the water had ordered his soldiers to come and drive out the French; and one day in the spring George Croghan asked that a council meet.

In the council he made a speech. The English and the Long Knives were starting, under a great general, to capture Fort Duquesne. The general had asked for warriors to help him.

Ugh! With all the Mingo warriors—fifty—and their families, Croghan set out to meet the General at Will's Creek. There were Scarouady and Silver Heels and White Thunder and Big Tree and the Buck, and Robert, and the rest, not omitting Bright Lightning.

Will's Creek has changed. A fort stood here now, named Fort Cumberland. And around the fort were a host of tents in lines, and red coats, and a batch of blue coats, horses, cattle, wagons and cannon on wheels.

It was a wonderful sight, and made Scarouady grunt approval.

"Ho!" he said. "Now I see the English. We shall eat up the French."

The soldiers sent by the King were in red, with high, black, shiny hats, and white cross belts, and white leggins buttoned below the knee, and hair twisted into stubby tails hanging down their backs; large and fierce they looked. They numbered one thousand. The red of one half had yellow trimmings; of the other half, clay.

The blue-coated soldiers were Long Knives; four hundred and fifty, in nine companies. There were soldiers from New York and from Carolina, too. And there were seamen, or sailors, from great ships. But these numbered only fifty. Their clothes were very odd, and so was their language.

The general or head chief was Sir Edward Braddock—a

famous warrior for the King. Gist was here, and so was Andrew Montour; and so were Captain Thomas Waggener and Ensign Peyroney who had been sorely wounded at Fort Necessity, and Doctor Craik, and several others—all Washington men, among the Virginians.

Much of this Robert learned little by little, for he could not see everything at once. First, how about Washington? Washington surely would be here, too, among the Long Knife Americans. But when Washington appeared, he was in red uniform, riding upon a fine horse, into the Indian camp. When he saw Scarouady and the Hunter and others that he knew, his face lighted.

"Brudder," Scarouady greeted. "We go to fight 'um French."

They shook hands all around. Then Washington spoke to Robert, with his brief smile:

"I thank you for the letter." He was always very polite. "You did bravely."

"You heard?" Robert stammered.

"I heard. You were wounded; now you are well. That is good. And I hear that Tanacharison is dead and Scarouady is Half-King."

"Tanacharison no fight; heart get weak," Scarouady grunted. "Me Half-King. Me bring warriors to fight for English. Wah! See my brudder in red, Long Knives in blue. My brudder no Long Knife?"

"I sit in the council of General Braddock who is the great chief of all," answered Washington. "But I will be in the fight when my brothers and the Long Knives help the red-coat soldiers whip the French out of Fort Duquesne."

It took Croghan and Gist to explain, later, that Washington was an aide, or assistant, to the great Chief Braddock, and marched by his side: a high honor.

"His Excellency the General bids me to say to Scarouady that the Mingos are welcome," continued Washington, to Robert. "He has heard that they are great warriors. They shall be well rewarded."

"I am American. I stay with Washington," Robert pleaded hopefully.

"No," replied Washington. "I stay with the General, for

he has asked me to. You shall be American, if you like, and help show the way with Gist and Scarouady and the Virginians. I'd rather do that myself," he added quickly.

After this there was much going on. General Braddock (who was a stout, heavy, red-faced old man) invited Scarouady and White Thunder and other chiefs to his tent. He gave presents and exchanged speeches, which Andrew Montour translated.

He had the drums beat and the fifes play, and the great guns fired; and sent a bullock to the camp, for a feast.

The Mingos invited the English to come over, and danced the war-dance for them. The English, very stiff in their red coats with high collars, and their white skin-tight breeches and their high, black hats, seemed to think that the Mingos were funny, and stared at them through pieces of glass fitted to one eye, and laughed and clapped their hands.

But the Mingos had only dressed for war, too. Their faces were painted red and black and yellow, their heads were shaven clean except for the tuft of greased scalp-lock, and their ears were hung with rings and pendants of shells. They were no funnier than the English themselves.

King Shingis and King Beaver and Chief Killbuck of the Delawares came in. They feasted, and talked with the General; and when they went away again they had promised to meet the English on the march, with many warriors. But Scarouady did not believe this.

"Their hearts are French," he said. "Now they will go to Duquesne. We should march fast, and strike."

The General took a long time to get ready. Then, on a sudden, he said that he could not feed so many warriors and women and children. Let ten warriors stay, to help him find the enemy; the other Mingos must go home.

When Croghan told Scarouady, Scarouady laughed.

"I think little of this old red-faced soldier chief," he uttered. "He has never been in the woods, and he listens to no advice from us who have. While he is eating and drinking and making his stiff-coated men walk about like bears on their hind legs, I could take my men and Washington could take his men and we could capture the French. But I will stay, for I wish to fight the French, and I will not desert Washington.

The rest may go home."

Most of the Mingos did go home. The men were glad enough to do so; they did not get along well with the English soldiers, who treated them like children and seemed to have no manners; and besides, they heard that Gist's son had been sent to bring up the Cherokees and Catawbas, who were enemies.

The women and children had been having a good time. Bright Lightning had been having the best time of all, for she was pretty and smart and was called a princess by the officers. But her father White Thunder sent her home with the others.

"You stay?" she asked of Robert and the Buck.

"We stay."

"Wah!" Bright Lightning laughed. "I would stay too if I were a warrior. But maybe when you get into Fort Duquesne I will come and get you out. The English chief thinks he can blind the French and Ottawa with his red coats, but they will cut him into pieces like a snake."

The Scarouady people went back to Aukwick. Those who did stay were Scarouady, White Thunder, Aroas who was Silver Heels, Big Tree, Cashuwayon or Captain Newcastle who was a Delaware and a son of old Queen Allaquippa, Scarouady's son-in-law Iagrea, Guyasuta the young warrior, the Buck and Robert the Hunter.

Yes, the red-faced General seemed to be an unwise man. On the very day before the start was made, who should come into camp but Captain Jack the Black Rifle, leading thirty of his white warriors, all dressed for war. Washington and Gist and others shook hands with him. He went into the Braddock tent, and did not stay long. Soon he came out and he motioned to his men, and they left in single file, to enter the forest again.

Then Scarouady shouted: "Ho! Black Rifle!" He and Croghan ran after, and so did the Buck and Robert, to hear.

"Listen!" exclaimed Scarouady. "You are men. We are brothers. Do the Black Rifles and the Mingo scout together against the French and Ottawa dogs? Good! Now I feel hope."

"No," said the Black Rifle. "The English chief sends us away. He has soldiers in red to fight in the woods for him."

The Black Rifle men hurried on.

Gist laughed angrily.

"Scarouady knows that the Black Rifle is worth five hundred red-coat soldiers who have never fought in the woods. The Black Rifle offered to serve without pay."

"I see that the chief called Braddock is like a buffalo bull," replied Scarouady. "Where he looks, there he will go, without reason. He sends away my fifty warriors; he sends away the Black Rifle. If he sends away Washington and the Long Knives, we are lost, for in the woods his red-coat soldiers will be like the gobbling turkey when the hunter watches."

After the long time getting prepared they all started to capture Fort Duquesne. This day was the tenth day of June, in the year Seventeen Hundred and Fifty-five. There were two thousand one hundred men. Six hundred men with axes and provision wagons and cannon had been ordered ahead to widen Washington's road from Will's Creek to Gist's place. The army followed, with Gist and Scarouady's men scouting in advance.

The march was very slow, because of the baggage and the great guns. The officers rode horses, and there was a small company of Long Knives called "Light Horse;" the other soldiers walked. Sometimes only two or three miles were covered in a day, and the line of men and wagons and cannon and pack horses reached from camp to camp.

Looking back through clearings, the Buck and Robert could see the march: a long, long column of wagons, cannon and horses, and on either side the red coats, and the fewer blue coats, all toiling up hill and down hill, through woods and bogs, with their weapons flashing and the thickly clothed English soldiers sweating as they carried their heavy muskets, knapsacks, cartridge boxes, tall hats and their stiff boots.

If their own scouts could see them so plainly, the enemy could see them, too. This proved to be true. The Buck came running back one evening and said that he and Scarouady had been seized by French and Indians, but that he had escaped to bring the news.

Then Gist, White Thunder, Newcastle, Aroas and the

Hunter all ran to rescue poor Scarouady if they could. There he was, tied to a tree. He said that the French were for killing him, but that Guyasuta had been with the Ottawas, and they refused to use the hatchet on a great chief.

Guyasuta did not turn up again. He had gone over to the French.

After this many signs of the French and Indians were seen, in shape of camp fires and of boasts written upon barked trees.

Still the column moved on, getting deeper and deeper into the wilderness. In the many rough places it reached back four miles, along the road only twelve feet wide. The soldiers from the King across the water never had seen this kind of a country—so big, so lone, so wet, so rocky, so dark with huge trees, so silent with watchful death. How they toiled and sweated, those red-coats! The mosquitoes bit them, the ticks burrowed into them, the rattlesnakes struck them, their feet blistered with walking and their hands blistered with tugging at the ropes and at the wagon and cannon wheels when the horses failed.

But at night they tried to be merry. Around their camp fires they sang a song which Robert heard often enough to remember.

> To arms, to arms! My jolly grenadiers!
> Hark, how the drums do roll it along!
> To horse, to horse, with valiant good cheer!
> We'll meet our proud foe, before it is long.
> Let not your courage fail you:
> Be valiant, stout and bold;
> And it will soon avail you,
> My loyal hearts of gold.
> Huzzah, my valiant countrymen! Again I say huzzah!
> 'Tis nobly done—the day's our own—huzzah, huzzah!
> March on, march on, brave Braddock leads the foremost;
> The battle is begun, as you may fairly see.
> Stand firm, be bold, and it will soon be over;
> We soon will gain the field from our proud enemy.

And so forth. A fine warrior song.

"They are foolish, but they are brave," even Scarouady admitted. "The woods are no place for them, just the same."

There had not been much opportunity to see Washington. He had given up his best horse to be used as a pack horse. Gist said that Washington, too, was worried over the long line that the French might cut to pieces, and over the slow march. He wished to speak to the General about hurrying.

He must have done so, for at the Little Meadows, about twenty-five miles from Will's Creek, a man named Colonel Dunbar was left with part of the heavy baggage and provisions and about one thousand men. Taking twelve hundred of the best men, and twenty cannon, and thirty wagons, General Braddock pushed on. Four hundred of these men were kept to the front, making the trail.

After another long time they all came to the Great Meadows; but they did not stop to look at Fort Necessity. They camped on the other side, and then marched up the Laurel Hills and camped near the Rock Fort where Washington and Tanacharison had met to attack Jumonville.

Robert remembered that night very well; so did Scarouady and so did Washington, probably—but Washington was not here now. He was sick and unable to travel.

That was bad. Washington was behind, with Colonel Dunbar. Still Gist had said:

"Have no fear. He stays to get well for the fight, by the General's orders. The General thinks so much of him that he promises to wait for him before striking the French."

The next camp was at Gist's place. The mountains had been crossed, but the forests were as dense as ever. The soldiers began to get nervous. They heard strange sounds at night; by day men straggling aside to pick berries were killed and scalped.

When the march was within twenty-five or thirty miles of Fort Duquesne by trail, and only thirteen by straight line, the Buck was killed also.

XVIII

A Little Bear In A Tree

Scarouady, White Thunder, Aroas, the Buck and Robert had been scouting in front. They had to be very careful. It was near evening, and they had turned back, when White Thunder saw figures stealing through the trees of a little dip.

"Hist!" he said. "There are Ottawa!"

And they, too, stole rapidly to head the Ottawa off. Then when they were running among the trees, here came soldiers, running too; and the soldiers halted and leveled their guns.

"Ho!" cried Scarouady. He stopped short and stood out and grounded his gun and held up a leafy bough that he tore from a bush. This was the sign agreed upon between the scouts and the soldiers, as a friend sign.

But the soldiers were excited. They paid no attention to the sign; their guns spoke, the bullets spatted, and the Buck fell. The soldiers saw their mistake too late. They saw it when Scarouady ran with a wild shout and looked at the Buck, and sat beside him with his hands over his face.

In a moment he uncovered his face. He drew his paint from his belt pouch and by the time the soldiers had come in he had painted his face black. That was the mourning color.

The soldiers were sorry and tried to explain, but this was no time to listen to them. As for Robert, he felt cold and sick. Instead of scolding the soldiers Scarouady uttered no word; he let them lift the Buck and carry him back to the camp. He and White Thunder, Aroas and the Hunter trod after.

Washington had just arrived at the camp, in a wagon. Thin and pale he was from his sickness. The wagon trip must have hurt him, but evidently he had been determined not to miss a battle.

His eyes saw the procession as it wended through among the soldiers; he read Scarouady's paint; and he hurried upon unsteady legs.

"What, brother! You wear the death paint!" he exclaimed.

"You see my son. He is dead by soldier bullets," said

Scarouady.

"How is that? Where is he?"

"He is with my people," said Scarouady. "I go to ask the great chief why he kills my son. Now I have no more to live for."

"What happened?" Washington asked of George Croghan, whom Scarouady had sent for.

Croghan told him. Washington closed his lips firmly, but he, too, made no complaint.

"Do you and Scarouady come with me," he uttered. "I will take you, myself, to General Braddock. It is unfortunate, unfortunate." And he added, to Scarouady: "Be brave, my brother. The Buck died as a warrior, serving our country."

Scarouady did not answer; he only followed after Washington and Croghan.

When he returned to where the rest of them were sitting with Gist, while Iagrea beat the deerskin drum and sang praises of the warrior Buck, he seemed to feel better.

"Is it well with you, Monacathuatha?" Gist asked, using Scarouady's other name as Half-King.

"One chief has talked to another," said Scarouady. "I have heard good words."

Then came Croghan and a squad of red-coat soldiers, under an officer, with a litter. They took the Buck to a tent, and put him in it on a bed, and a guard of soldiers walked before it.

After supper the Buck was buried by soldiers. Many officers shook Scarouady's hand; General Braddock was there, and Washington, and the other head men. When the Buck had been covered up soldiers fired volleys over him— to drive off the evil spirits, said White Thunder, but Croghan explained that the guns were soldier honors, announcing the burial of a brave warrior.

This camp was named Monacathuatha, in Scarouady's honor, and should always be known as such. All that pleased Scarouady.

"I can see that the Buffalo (who was Braddock) has a good heart," he said, after everything had been done. "But he should not send his red-coat men alone into the woods. They have no eyes. Now my son is lost to me. The Washington men would have looked before they shot."

Pretty soon Washington came with Andrew Montour and Doctor Craik to sit by the fire. Washington had put off his red coat and was in buckskin hunting-shirt, like a Long Knife Ranger.

"Wah!" Scarouady approved. "My brudder no turkey gobbler on bare limb. He a panther in the bushes."

"You are feeling stronger, colonel?" Gist asked. "We rejoice to have you at the front again."

"Somewhat stronger," Washington answered. "I would not for five hundred pounds have missed a battle, so I travelled up by wagon as I found myself unable to sit a horse."

"He should be in bed," said Doctor Craik. "But I can do nothing with him." Then the merry doctor laughed. "Nor he with Braddock. I should hate to have two such patients."

"You find the General difficult to advise, I take it, colonel," said Gist. "Since you have been behind we have moved on like a tortoise—as you know. At this gait I feared we would spend the rest of our life in the woods."

"The General has stopped to bridge every little stream and level every mole-hill, despite the danger that the French might be reinforced meantime," said Washington. "But it has not been my place to advise unless requested; my rank as captain does not entitle me to that, and I am only a Provincial."

"But with experience in this kind of country, and against that kind of enemy, colonel," Croghan retorted. "You have taken matters into your own hand and changed your garb, at least, I see."

"Yes," said Washington. "I did go so far as to suggest to my friends among the officers that we all adopt woodsman clothes instead of the flaming red, as less easier targets; and reminded them of Mr. Benjamin Franklin's remark, when at Fort Cumberland: 'The finer the feathers, the better for the fowler.' But they assured me that the General would never permit it—he would call it unworthy of the King's soldiers. I have been no little jeered at for my own prudence, but I see no virtue in needless exposure either of men or armies."

"By that token, then, His Excellency will still insist upon

beating up the enemy with his red-coat Regulars who can be seen for five miles, rather than use the Virginia woodsmen," Gist grumbled.

"As we will soon be within touch of the fort," replied Washington, "and are liable to surprise, for our approach is surely known, I did make bold to suggest to the General that he now permit me to take my Virginia Rangers and scout well to the fore. And I explained to him that these men were accustomed to the Indian mode of warfare and would be of utmost service in protecting his advance column from ambush. But this idea of relying upon what he was pleased to term 'half-drilled farmers' to protect the King's Regulars appeared to anger him, so I said no more. Besides, he was so good as to state for my further understanding that Lieutenant-Colonel Gage has been promised the honor of the advance, with a detachment of picked grenadiers and one company of the New York Regulars and would probably resent being displaced by raw Provincials."

"Then what use is to be made of the Rangers, I wonder?" said Gist.

"They are to be employed as a rear guard, to protect the baggage, I believe."

"And I believe, that unless you would be consigned to the rear guard yourself, colonel, you should go to bed at once and gain strength," laughed Doctor Craik. "Now, sir! Are you one to take advice or not?"

"As I have no mind to be anywhere near the rear in time of action—good night, gentlemen," Washington said promptly. He rose. "I have talked only as among friends, with no thought of criticizing His Excellency General Braddock. He is an experienced soldier, of distinguished record——"

"But not in our style of fighting, colonel," put in Gist. "This is not settled Europe; it is the American wilderness, as you know."

"Nevertheless he is trained to arms, and is of great courage, and will fight. He is certain that the French Indians will not face our cannon and the bayonets of the British Regulars; and neither will the few French. We have not been attacked as yet, and here we are, almost within striking distance. In fact, very likely our showing will induce the fort to surrender without a blow. I wish the neighborhood of the fort had been a little better scouted upon, and so does he; but I realize the difficulty of anyone leaving the column without being observed by spies and cut off."

"Well, we will do our duty and hope for the best," said Doctor Craik. "And if there's no work for the surgeon, here's one who will be satisfied. Now, colonel, my duty is to place you in bed."

With that, he put his arm through Washington's and led him away. Captain Montour, Croghan and Gist talked together. The red-coat soldiers were singing again, around their fires:

> See how, see how, they break and fly before us!
> See how they are scattered over all the plain!
> Now, now—now, now, our country will adore us!
> In peace and in triumph, boys, when we return again!
> And the chorus, with everybody joining in:
> Huzzah, my valiant countrymen! Again I say huzzah!
> 'Tis nobly done—the day's our own—huzzah, huzzah!

"Wah!" said Scarouady. "They sing to the woods, and the woods have ears. Braddock does not send the Long Knives on the scout, though they are many. He sends us, who are few; and he sends his red-coat bears, who shoot us. He asks us to go closer to the French fort, and spy; and then we will have the French and Ottawa and Huron all around us and the red-coat fools behind us. Very well; early in the morning I will take Aroas and go to spy on the French fort. I will show him that my heart is good toward him, for he has taken me by the hand like a man. I will show him and Washington that Scarouady can be strong in sorrow. When I have washed off my mourning paint with scalps I shall feel better."

So saying, Scarouady drew his blanket over his head, and lay down as if to sleep.

Pretty soon the others went to sleep, although Robert stayed awake a little time thinking of the Buck. He was going to miss the Buck, who had been like a brother to him. But if Scarouady could face the grief, he ought to, also. Scarouady certainly was a fine man.

The Hunter dozed off; he slept—and he was awakened by Gist's hand upon his shoulder and Gist's voice in his ear.

"Come."

"Where?"

"We are going on a scout, too. Scarouady and Aroas are already gone."

Robert threw off his blanket and sat up and grabbed his gun.

"To the French fort?"

"Yes. Or as near as we can get. They two, now we two."

Wah! That promised sport. He and Gist were to see if they could not find out more than Scarouady and Aroas could. So he sprang to his feet and followed Christopher Gist out of the sleeping group. A sentry muffled in a great-coat and looking like a bear indeed leveled his gun and said something; Gist answered with a word, and they passed on into the woods.

The sky was not yet gray, but the air seemed to have thinned a little, so that morning was not far removed. Gist trotted rapidly, munching a piece of meat; and Robert trotted in his steps, munching likewise.

It was a good hour. The woods were silent. The Forks of the Ohio where the French fort lay were only thirteen miles across country; and Gist knew the way as well as Robert did. By daylight they should be near enough to it to use their eyes; then if the coast were clear they could hide, and go on in the evening, and spy again in the early morning, and get back.

So they trotted rapidly. After a time the dusk had paled and birds were twittering. They kept on. The sun rose, and still they kept on. They had seen nobody and nobody had seen them. It looked as though they might get almost to the fort— maybe they could see it.

The fort now could not be far ahead. Robert thought that he heard axes chopping, away, 'way before. Sounds carried a long distance. They two stole forward, more cautiously. Yes, those were axes; and that was a faint shout.

Surely the French at the fort feared nothing. Where were their scouts? Then, just as they two were topping a hill from which they ought to look down upon the Forks, sharp and swift there broke the crack of a rifle, ringing through the woods.

Gist halted. He knew that rifle-crack; so did the Hunter.

"That's Scaddy's barker; I can tell it among a thousand," said Gist. "He's after a scalp. Pshaw! Is he crazy? Now the woods will be alive. You wait here. I'll spy ahead and see what's what. If I'm chased, never mind me; take care of yourself, and go back to the camp."

On went Gist, and disappeared in the timber at the top of the hill. Now the air beyond, toward the fort, was tremulous with yells. Scarouady had waked the enemy; the Ottawas and Hurons were pouring out. The Hunter stood listening. Where was Gist? He had no notion of going back without Christopher Gist; but this place was rather open to wait in.

He was near a big white-oak tree. Why not climb into that? Then he would be off the ground, and he might see around better. Wah! Hark! Those were pursuit whoops! The French Indians were upon a warm trail! They seemed to be coming, too!

The Hunter leaned his heavy flint-lock against the white-oak trunk, and sprang for the lowest branch. The woods were echoing to the shouts. He had hauled himself up and was about to turn and reach down for his gun, when the shouts burst louder; the brush crackled—Gist passed, running and darting, at one side, and while the Hunter held motionless, waiting, two Ottawas sped like hounds right under the tree, eager to cut the trail.

They did not see the gun, which was behind the tree trunk. Were more Indians to follow? The Hunter gently tried for his gun, and could not quite reach it. Listen! Would he have time to get down? No! He kicked at the gun and it fell flat, to lie as if it had been dropped; and he started to climb higher, out of sight, for there were Indians all about.

Then he stopped short, frozen where he was; for he heard the soft thud of moccasins. He did not dare to turn his head and look. After a moment the sound ceased. He could hear nothing, and he simply had to look.

Through the leaves and branches he could glimpse an Indian under the tree. The Indian had discovered the gun, and was gazing about. Perhaps he would go on. Robert certainly hoped so. The Indian's eyes wandered up into the tree. He did not appear to see anybody there. They swept the ground again—hah! They began to read the prints there! They travelled back to the tree trunk—they saw something—maybe a place where the bark had been freshly torn by the gun-barrel, or by Robert's kicks when he climbed or knocked over the gun.

Ugh! The Indian gradually raised his face, his eyes travelled on up—he made discovery again—his rifle pointed; and the Hunter found himself gazing down into the muzzle and into the painted, wrinkled face behind it of old King Shingis the Delaware.

Shingis knew him, and commenced to grin.

"Ho, little bear!" he chuckled. "Come down. Acorns not ripe yet."

Well, Robert the Hunter came down. He thought it possible to land upon his gun, but Shingis had quickly picked that up and knocked out the flint.

"Ugh!" said Shingis, receiving him with a grip in his hair. "Fine little bear. But tree a bad place. Many hunters around. Look for Mingo bear. Better be Delaware bear. Go to fort with Shingis. Shingis got no boy. Now he take care of this boy. Make him Delaware."

So saying, Shingis gave a series of whoops; other Indians came running—they laughed, and tying the Hunter's arms hustled him on to the fort.

The pursuit sounds had died away. Christopher Gist may have won free, and so he had; for, as Robert afterward found out, Gist and Scarouady and Aroas as well, got back to the column—Scarouady with the scalp of a French officer whom he had shot in the woods.

XIX
In Fort Duquesne Again

This was tough. There was a lot of whooping and shouting when from the edge of the clearing over which floated the white flag of France above the log walls old Shingis uttered his prisoner yell; and there was a lot of joking and laughing—and disappointment, too—when he marched his prisoner in and they all saw that it was nobody but a boy.

But hold! What boy? Why, the boy who had run away last fall! Wah! Ugh! Hurons and Pontiac's Ottawas recognized this boy; and Pontiac himself strode, scowling, to demand the prisoner of old Shingis.

Shingis and Pontiac had an argument about the matter. Then that seemed settled. Pontiac called, the Indians ran about grabbing things, and formed a long, double line, of men and women facing inward equipped with clubs and switches. The double line extended like a living lane to the fort gates.

The Hunter was to be punished by running the gantlet. He had to run through that lane while everybody took a whack at him as he passed; but when he came to the other end he was safe. Unless he was smart he would be well beaten.

Old Shingis plucked knife and hatchet from him, and shoved him forward to the entrance to the lane. Pontiac was watching.

"Now we see how fast a little bear runs," said King Shingis. "Go in Mingo; come out Delaware, get hurt no more. Run!" And with another shove would have started him off.

But the Hunter had not waited to be shoved. In a great bound he had torn free and had ducked past the first two or three double files, who missed him entirely with their switches. On he sped, ducking, dodging, diving—stung with switches and battered at by hasty clubs, amid wild shouts and laughter.

He was more than half way when he dimly saw his chance. Just ahead an old Indian was waiting straddled and bent over, to land a good blow upon him. The Hunter suddenly ducked lower; right under between the old Indian's legs he dived—up rose the Indian, down he came, but the Hunter was beyond, and outside the gantlet and scudding like a deer for those gates.

The lane scattered. A few of the Indians ran to head him off and hit him. These he dodged; they and the other Indians were not much in earnest now, anyway; he tore through a little knot of men at the gate and was inside. He had gained sanctuary, but when he stopped for breath he felt that he had been given a sound thrashing just the same, and had twisted his ankle. Maybe Pontiac would be satisfied with all that.

French officers were saying: "Smart little boy! Brave leetle fellow," in French and English. Then he heard another voice in English:

"Hurt you?"

He looked. This was a white boy, about his size but maybe somewhat older, rather battered up and limping with a stick.

"No," Robert answered.

"Come along with me. I'll fix you," the white boy bade.

He took the Hunter (hobbling proudly) to a house where there were medicines and a French doctor. The house was called a hospital. Here the few cuts from the clubs and switches were greased, but the cuts did not amount to much. He said nothing about his ankle.

The white boy's name was James Smith. He too had been captured—had been captured in the woods of Pennsylvania and brought here; had had to run the gantlet, but had not got off so easily as Robert.

Now for a second time Robert found himself in Fort Duquesne of the French, and wondering how he was to get out. Nobody appeared to pay much attention to him, but the whole place was much excited, as if not knowing what to do. The army of English and Long Knives was coming.

The French and the Indians of course knew this. Spies were keeping watch; Indians were constantly passing in through the gates, with word of the English, and French parties hastened out to scout the trails. For the Hunter to get back to Gist and Scarouady and Washington might be difficult.

He saw Guyasuta, but Guyasuta pretended not to notice

him and he put in most of the daytime with James Smith. James had been here for a week and more and had picked up much information.

The French officers were not the same as last fall. Contrecoeur who had driven Ward away was still commander; his captains were now men named Beaujeu, Dumas, and Ligneris. Langlade, the half-Ottawa, was here too; while inside and outside the fort there were the Indians— more kinds than the Hunter had ever seen together before.

A great many from the Big Lakes of the north—French Iroquois, the Hurons, Potawatomis, Ojibwas and Ottawas; besides Wyandots and Delawares and Shawnees and Mingos from the Ohio Country; all in their best costumes of bright blankets, fringed leggins, and beaded or quilled moccasins, and red, yellow and blue paint, with strips of black also.

Black Hoof of the Shawnees was here; Shingis, Beaver and Killbuck of the Delawares; Pontiac, the war chief of the Ottawas, and old Nissowaquet, head chief of all the Ottawas, whose sister was Langlade's wife; Anastase, head chief of the Hurons; oh, a score of famous chiefs, all helping the French.

Outside there were games and feasting and much loafing about; inside, the French soldiers drilled and stood guard and loafed, as though the English army was not feared. Nevertheless it was feared.

"These French know they can't fight off Braddock's men and cannon," said James Smith. "I've guessed that. They're layin' low and foxin' so the Injuns won't run away. The Injuns are scared, you bet."

He was glad to learn from Robert that the army was indeed very strong.

This evening there was a council of the French and the Indians, to talk things over. On his way to the council Shingis passed the Hunter and James. He grinned, and he said:

"Ugh! Pretty soon English come. March like fools, all togedder. Easy see 'um. French an' Injun shoot 'um all down like one pigeon. What white boy an' leetle Delaware think of that; huh?"

That did not sound good. But in the morning it looked as if the council had not agreed, for the French did not march out, and neither did the Indians. They still waited, and the

French officers acted rather glum. Captain Beaujeu (who was a handsome young man, slim and pink-cheeked) spent considerable time among the chiefs. He appeared to be arguing with them, and talking with Langlade.

This afternoon, when James Smith was sleeping and Robert was sitting alone, trying to figure upon getting away, Guyasuta came at last and sat beside him.

"Too bad you here," said Guyasuta in the Seneca. "Maybe you want to go."

"You fight the English, Guyasuta?" the Hunter asked.

"I fight the English," said Guyasuta. "That big red-coat general does not know how to treat Indians. He sends for us, then he sends us away. He treats us like children, and so do his red-coat soldiers. I will not march around by his orders. But I do not fight Washington and Scarouady. They are my brothers. You can tell them so."

"That is good, but how can I tell them?" answered Robert—with excellent reason.

"Yes," said Guyasuta; "you ran off from here once and the Ottawa are mad. Now Shingis would make you his son. You are Delaware. You will have hard work to run off again. Wait and we will see."

"I will wait till the English and the Long Knives come to take the fort; and that won't be long," replied Robert. "Then the French and their Indians will run, themselves."

"Wah!" said Guyasuta. "Maybe. It is a great army, with big guns. I know, because I saw it; everybody knows. The council hasn't decided what to do. There is another council tonight. The French are too few yet. The Indians ask the French captain how he expects their eight hundred men to whip four thousand with great guns. You must not try to run off. You had better wait. And I ask you not to tell that white boy that you have seen me. If I am known to be your friend then you will be shut up."

"He goes with me," said Robert, at once.

"Then you would be caught sure," replied Guyasuta. "He is white, and he is too lame to run. Besides, he will be well treated. The Delaware keep him to adopt him, for they like him."

Another council was held this night. The English army

had been sighted nearer, and the excitement in the fort had increased. From the council room there sounded loud speeches, by the French and by the chiefs.

"What do you make of it, Rob?" Jim asked. "Is that war? You're part Injun—you ought to know."

"I don't think so," Robert answered. "Sounds like two minds, one yes, one no. Injuns are scared."

When the council had quit there still were no signs of getting ready to fight: no running about inside; no war dances outside in the Indian camp.

After sunrise still another council was held, this time upon the ground not far from the very gates. Beaujeu the Canadian Ranger was there; and Langlade, Pontiac, Black Hoof, Killbuck, Beaver, Shingis and Anastase who had been chosen head chief of all. The warriors crowded forward, to listen; words rose high. Beaujeu and Langlade pleaded, but the Ottawas, the Hurons, the Delawares, the Iroquois, even the Shawnees, held back.

Anastase finally stood, and dropped his blanket again.

"No," he cried to Beaujeu. "We have told you that Onontio ought not to ask his children to die for him. Does my young father wish to die? It is not the part of wise men to fight four thousand with a few hundred. We know that the Mingos do not want this fort here, so why should we uselessly try to hold it for the French? We shall not march to certain death. The French should have brought more men."

"Ugh! Look!"

A runner was pelting down from the woods for the fort. He came on across the cleared ground—he came with news and he arrived sweaty and panting.

The English army had forded a bend of the Monongahela below the old Fraser trading house! They were marching through the bend, to ford again above, near Fraser's, only ten miles from the fort. They would be here soon, with all their soldiers and their great guns.

The council broke into a tumult and a hurrying about. No one seemed to know what to do. Then up sprang Beaujeu— and a gallant young figure he was, too, his head bare, his yellow hair floating, his eyes very blue and his face flushed.

"Listen!" he shouted. "Are you women? Do I see you

afraid? The English are at the river. Now is the time. Let us meet them on our own ground, where one man can stop twenty. Listen! I am resolved to meet them. It shames me to stay here. What! Will you let your father go alone against the enemy? Come, for he is certain of success."

Those were the right words at the right moment. Who could resist the brave Beaujeu? A great yell answered him. Chief after chief shook his hand.

"Only wait. We will follow our father."

Beaujeu ran inside. Soldiers hurried out, rolling barrels of powder and casks of bullets, and knocked the heads in, before the gates. Chiefs and warriors were painting; they paused only long enough to cluster around the barrels and casks and to scoop their powder flasks and bullet pouches full. Inside, orders were being shouted, and soldiers were lining up. It was to be war in the woods.

With James Smith, Robert the Hunter had been looking down upon this scene from the top of the palisade wall near the gates. Here they two clung; and in the excitement he had forgotten Jim, but now he heard him.

"They're going to attack!"

"Yes. Surprise."

"Where, you think?"

"Maybe at second ford. Good place, where army crosses second time, to get on this side."

"How far?"

"Maybe ten mile, by trail to Fraser place."

"You know?"

Robert nodded.

"Then you run, Rob. Tell 'em."

"Leave you, Jim?"

"Yes. I've got to stay. I'm lame. Couldn't get away anyhow. But you can look like an Injun."

Just then Robert heard a hiss. Guyasuta had passed along under him. And he saw that Jim was very white, and weak, and had hard work even to hang to the palings. Washington must be warned! Guyasuta had signalled; so the Hunter only said "goodbye" and he dropped down and followed Guyasuta.

XX
The Battle In The Woods

Guyasuta led right on to an inside angle of the log walls, and there he stopped, behind a building where few could see.

"Now!" he said, when Robert joined him; and he opened a little package that he took from his pouch. "I will make a French Mohawk of you. You can march with them who do not know you in the Mohawk paint. Then maybe you can get ahead of the ambush and find Washington and Scarouady."

"What do you do?" asked the Hunter.

"I war with the English. If the red-coats caught me now they would kill me. But you can tell Washington and Scarouady to look out."

With his sharp knife Guyasuta slashed off Robert's brown hair close to the head and left only a Mohawk scalp-lock. He rubbed reddish grease into the fuzzy crown and daubed the scalp-lock black and red so that it lay stiffly; and he rapidly painted Robert's face with red and black; and when Robert had slipped off his buckskin shirt he painted his brown chest and arms.

"Here are hatchet and knife, and powder flask and bullet pouch," said Guyasuta. "You will find plenty gun outside. Go quickly. I do this because my heart is good toward Washington and Scarouady, and you and I are brothers too."

"Wah!" uttered the Hunter. "I go."

Then looking like a young Mohawk warrior, for he was straight and well formed, Robert the Hunter boldly ran to the gate and went out among the other Indians bustling to and fro.

All were still painting and arming—jostling to seize the guns piled ready for the taking, and to fill up with powder and lead.

Robert glanced at the top of the wall near the gate. He saw Jim there, clinging fast; and Jim looked down upon him and did not recognize him! Nobody paid any attention to him amid the excitement.

Within the fort drums had been rolling, commands were

being shouted. Soldiers stood in line. Here came Beaujeu, in Indian buckskin shirt and leggins and moccasins, upon his head a soft, black hat with brim fastened up at one side by an eagle feather, upon his chest a dangling silver brooch as sign that he was an officer. He was to lead.

The Hunter kept away from the Delawares and the Pontiac Ottawas. His heart beat high, for he yet might be known through his paint. Where were the Mohawks? There they were, getting together, with the French Iroquois their brothers; and he hastened over and sat down, to wait the signal of the chiefs.

Ho! There went Beaujeu, turning with a shout—"Here, my children!"—and with gallant wave of hat. After him trotted the Anastase Hurons. The Mohawk and Caugh-na-wa-ga chiefs cried: "Quick! Or the Hurons shame us!" and with a great yell the jealous Mohawks and other Iroquois leaped to join the van before the Ottawas and Shawnees beat them.

The Delawares and Mingos had stood aside. They were not yet decided; and they stayed at the fort.

Seemingly as eager as any, Robert trotted with the Mohawks. Nobody had eyes for him; he was a warrior in full paint, like the rest of them. The Hurons travelled rapidly, taking a long, single file when they entered the woods; the Mohawks and Caugh-na-wa-gas also travelled rapidly, taking to single file. By the yells behind, the other bands were following. Then the forest swallowed the noise.

Pat-pat, scuff-scuff, sounded the moccasins. The attack from ambush along the trail of the English and Long Knives had started into motion. Robert the Hunter, in Mohawk paint, wondered how he was to get out of the scrape in time to find the red-coat column—but it would be better first to find Scarouady, or Gist, or the Virginians, and send word to Washington.

By the talk, now and then, the English were to be attacked at the second ford of the Monongahela. That was ten miles by rough trail. Wah! He did not know whether he could keep up this pace, for his strained ankle was hurting cruelly. If he could drop out, some way, and cut across, he could shorten the distance; and he'd have to wash off that paint or he'd be shot on sight by an English bullet.

Ho! And ever pat-pat, scuff-scuff, on the way to surprise Washington! Ho! He could make good use of that ankle. He began to limp more than necessary; and soon the Mohawk next behind him said:

"My young brother is lame. Let me go ahead."

"Pebble in my moccasin," Robert replied gladly. So he fell out and sat down, to rid himself of that pebble. While he was pretending to take his moccasin off the file passed.

"Wah! My brother will be late for scalps," said the last Caugh-na-wa-ga.

"I will catch up," answered Robert, still fussing. And the trotting file disappeared around a bend. Now Robert sprang to his feet, cast one glance to see that the coast was clear, and dived into the brush.

He could not nurse his ankle any more. But he had left the trail to Fraser's and the river, and the going was worse.

Viny ravines blocked him, and tangled or rocky slopes slowed him; and what with his hurry and his many detours he almost lost his way. Besides, his ankle did hurt, whether he minded or not. Then he came to a spring, and he stopped just long enough to scrub the paint from his face and chest with wet clay. Then he ran on, feeling better. He was no French Mohawk now; he was a Washington man.

Wah! He had washed off his paint too soon! What was that? He heard voices—he had approached the trail again; no, this was a little side trail, and all around him lay a park which he dared not cross while those voices were so near. He acted as quick as thought—he thrust his gun under a log and shinned full speed into a tree. He scarcely had climbed well up, and held rigid, when more Indians arrived.

They were Ottawas, trotting like wolves, with Pontiac leading; after them came the Potawatomis under Langlade, and the Ojibwas, and the Shawnees of Black Hoof; and after these came the woodsmen Rangers in their hunting clothes, and a company of French regular soldiers in blue and white. Who next? The Hunter figured that he had seen over six hundred Indians and almost three hundred French upon the march to war.

While he hung in his tree he looked abroad to figure just where he was. It was a fine big tree upon a hill. He could see the Monongahela, down toward Fraser's; not very far, either, by air line—and the bend of the river flashed back at him with moving figures.

The English army was crossing! Ho, what a sight through the sunshine! In solid red line it was crossing, and the flags flew, and by the glitter of the instruments the bands were making music—he could see even the white cross-belts of the grenadiers, beneath the tall, peaked, black-leather hats; the officers rode alongside their companies, and their swords glanced brightly when they waved orders.

The cannon were tugged through; and the wagons and the cattle and the pack horses splashed high; and the Long Knife Americans marched, in their buckskins and their blue, guarding the rear. There were scouts out, too, up stream and down stream—grenadiers. And at last—huzzah!—the whole army was across. The French and Indians were too late to stop it there!

As nobody came, Robert dropped out of his tree, and grabbed up his gun and ran again. He might yet be in time, while Beaujeu was planning another ambush.

He went scudding on, down hill and up, on short cut once more, to reach Washington and tell him; he had gone maybe half way from the tree to Fraser's near the river when "Crack! Crack! Crackity-crack crack! Bang! Bangity bang! Bang-bang-bang! Bang-g-g-g!" the woods shook! The battle! He himself was too late.

Just how Robert arrived at the scene he did not know. He must have run very fast, for the first thing he did know he was right into the yelling and the shooting and the smoke—and the French Indians!

These were the Hurons, hiding behind trees and logs and bushes, or darting around from cover to cover, while they shot. He just saw Beaujeu, leaping like a deer and cheering in French while he waved to the Canadian Rangers to come on. And on before, through the trees, there showed a mass of red—the coats of the English, who stood in the trail. Then from the red there belched a great cloud, and another thunderous volley, crashing through the woods. The bullets whined among the branches, as if the English were aiming too high; but down fell Beaujeu, and down sprawled several

Hurons, dead.

A cry rose from the French Rangers. They were running away, crying: "Save yourself! Save yourself!" But another French officer sprang out, calling them back. The English in red coats were pressing on, through the narrow trail of freshly felled trees, and what they cried was: "Huzzah! Huzzah! God save the King!"

Then the English column parted, two cannon spoke with tremendous noise, and a storm of bullets rushed through the trees, splintering the bark and cutting off branches. At that terrible thunder and lightning the Indians ran also, to one side and another; and Robert likewise scuttled, for the cannons were to speak again, this time into the face of a great volley from more French soldiers who had come on.

More red-coats were coming, too, at the double-quick, from down the slope. But the Indians had not run far. They were spread on both sides of the narrow road: they were hiding in hollows and ravines, where the pea-vines grew thickly and the trees clustered, and were shooting and yelling.

Next, Robert found himself among the Potawatomis. And still he edged along, seeking to get around and find a way in to Washington.

The woods all about him were full of darting, crawling, shrieking painted figures, scarcely to be seen amid the brush and the smoke. The noise was dreadful, while the English volleys answered the French volleys, and the great guns boomed, and the muskets and rifles of the Indians whanged without a pause.

Now and then he could see the English soldiers; they were surging this way, and that way, shooting without aim into the trees, while their officers beat their muskets down with swords or tried to wave a charge. Pretty soon he seemed to have reached the end of the Indians on this side of the road. And suddenly a Shawnee right before him leaped high, with a death yell; and while several other Indians in covert here broke and legged for safety, rifles cracked to stop them and a tall chief—followed by his men, among them a white man— raced in for the scalp.

Robert lunged forward, regardless. His shout was drowned in the scalp halloo of Scarouady; he tripped and fell, and next the hatchet of Scarouady was poised over his shaved head. Only just in time he wriggled aside, and flung up his arm and showed his face.

"No, no! See me, Scarouady!" he gasped.

"Wah!" panted Scarouady. "The Hunter! I saw a Mohawk scalp!"

Nothing more could be said now. Bullets sang past; Scarouady leaped for the Shawnee scalp, and he and Aroas, Gist, Iagrea, Newcastle and White Thunder "treed" again, to hold their ground.

The Hunter crept to Gist.

"Where've you been? You've turned Mohawk?" said Gist, between shots. "Why is that?"

"Shingis took me to fort," the Hunter panted. "Guyasuta there. He turned me Mohawk to get me out. Where is Washington, Gist?"

"In the thick of it, I'll wager," rapped Gist. "Will you go to him?"

"Yes."

"Good! But you can't go in that Injun garb. Buckskin wouldn't save you, either. The red-coats shoot at every moving thing. Wait here." And Gist rapidly crawled away, darted from tree to tree and disappeared in the smoke.

He came back with a round hat and a round jacket; they were bloody, they had been worn by a wood chopper and Gist was bleeding, too, from a ball that had scraped his ear.

"On with these. You'll have to make a run for it. The woods are full of death—those Injuns are everywhere. Find the colonel. Tell him I say to fetch on the Virginians; make those red-coats take to the trees; Braddock has got to fight Injun fashion or he'll not have a soldier left. Run."

Robert ran. He was seen—the bullets pinged after—they crossed his course—they fanned his cheeks, they seared his eyes, they ripped through his coat and hat; whether he was struck he did not know, although he thought he felt a sharp blow and a pain in one arm; but he left Gist and Scarouady and the little squad trying to keep the enemy at bay on this flank, and plunging on through the drifted smoke he emerged into the road.

This was turmoil, with soldiers stumbling down, some

hatless, some wounded, all bewildered; and with soldiers marching up, pressing on cheering, their officers leading, until the crowd from up the slope met them and rammed in through them, for cover; and then there was another hurly-burly.

Even here on the outskirts Robert was shoved to and fro. A galloping horse knocked him over. He got up. The soldiers from below had formed again; they marched in a solid line, with their bayonets pointed, and a fine officer in scarlet and gold in front of them, to charge the hill. But the bullets crumpled them, and their tall hats flew, and they stopped as if a strong wind were blowing against them; and in a moment their officer was marching alone. So he had to come back.

Here, on the run, came part of the Virginia Long Knives, at last; they ran at double-quick, through the trees—the blue facing on their buckskin shirts twinkled amid the green leaves and the pale smoke. Washington had not waited, then! But where was Washington? There—galloping in amid the red-coat soldiers, swinging his hat and huzzahing. Robert made for him—arrived just as he was off his horse.

Washington had been riding upon a pillow; the pillow stayed on the saddle—he tossed the reins one side—"Hold this horse, somebody!" he rasped, and Robert grabbed the reins. Washington appeared to pay no attention, for he ran to one of the cannon, helped to point it into a ravine and fire it and load it.

Now he was here, there, everywhere, with Robert trying to follow him and lead the rearing horse. No easy job this, while the bullets whined and men were falling. A horse made a good target, too.

The grenadier soldiers were being forced back. They stood in groups—officers snatched flags and bore them forward and waved the men on, but the men could not follow. They seemed to see nothing at which to aim—their red faces were sweaty, their eyes were wild, and they fired their muskets into the air. But they were brave; they stood, to be shot down.

More soldiers arrived, to crowd the road; and more Virginians, to take to the trees. Suddenly Washington seized the lines from the Hunter's hands and leaped into the saddle (the pillow had tumbled off) and tore through the red masses.

Washington Was Here, There, Everywhere

General Braddock was here; and he, too, was galloping right and left, shouting and swinging his sword and urging the men to the colors. Some of the soldiers had taken to the trees, like the Long Knives. But General Braddock was driving them out, with his sword, into the road again. "Cowards," he roared—he was a furious bear. "Cowards! Out, or I kill ye!"

The Hunter heard some of this, for he had followed Washington. He intended to stick by Washington. And Washington was correcting the General and pointing to the Virginians among the trees. But General Braddock would have none of that.

Down fell the General's horse. He seized another. Down fell Washington's horse. He seized another; there were holes through his clothing, made by bullets. Thomas Waggener, who had been at the Jumonville fight and at Fort Necessity, came at double-quick with almost a hundred Virginia "Blues" in buckskin, their guns at a trail; and they dropped behind a huge log, at one side of the road; then their guns belched smoke and ball into the Indians; then a company of the grenadiers saw the smoke and all fired into it; and the Long Knives had to run out or be shot in the back.

It was curious how many things one sees when one is excited! And that was the way with Robert, lost in the noise and the jostling, and turning now this way, now that, to keep track of Washington.

Washington was upon a third horse! Braddock was being helped upon another, also. Washington appeared to be the only officer left near him. The Indians were screeching ever more gladly; and as fast as the soldiers were blown backward by the blasts of bullets, the screeches and shots clung to them on either side.

Now everybody was upon a piece of bottom-land, down toward the river. The English were still firing without aim from the narrow road; the Virginians were keeping to the trees; Washington was following the General, as if begging him to let the red-coats join the Long Knives and fight as they fought. A gray-haired old English officer (whose name was Halket) hurried to argue also with the General; but they all were being carried backward still by the soldiers.

Then down fell the gray-haired officer; then a young officer, his son, jumped to lift him, and down fell the son. Then the soldiers moved faster and faster, and they began to run, throwing away their guns, with Washington and the

General and several other officers spreading their arms and beating with their swords to stop them.

But it was no use. Robert ran too, for the road was like a stream. He had to run, or be swept down and trampled upon. There was shooting from either side, and shooting behind, and the Virginians were still darting from tree to tree, answering with their guns. But the red-coat soldiers seemed to have shot all their ammunition—and not to much purpose, either.

After a short time he came out of the boiling current into a little eddy formed by an oak tree overhanging the road. Washington was here, with two other officers, bending over General Braddock.

General Braddock was not so angry of face, now; he was paling, and blood was welling from his right arm and his chest. He had been shot through, and could scarcely speak. It looked to be a bad wound. A brave man, this. Robert afterward heard that he had five horses killed under him before he himself was struck.

The soldiers were pouring past, and paid no attention. Not one stopped, for the Indians were yelling the scalp yells. The two officers with Washington ran out and ordered and pleaded; then they stopped a little cart; they carried the General to it, and put him upon it, and trundled him on.

Washington turned about. He saw the Hunter, and he looked astonished.

"What are you doing here? Go to safety!"

"I stay with Washington," Robert answered.

"Then you shall work. Find me my horse. We must help my Virginians hold the enemy from the ford."

Washington ran forward. Every loose horse had been seized by the soldiers, who galloped right over Robert. So he followed Washington again, who was trying to halt the soldiers, and make them join the Virginians. Doctor Craik came on, helping a wounded officer.

The Virginians were holding the rear and the woods at the foot of the hill. The Indians were pressing them closely. Had it not been for the Long Knife Americans in blue buckskin many of these soldiers never would have reached the ford. And likely the Indians would have crossed and killed all between the fords.

But the Long Knives kept falling back, from tree to tree. Colonel Washington was with them now, ordering and urging: "Stand firm, lads! Waste no shot. Brave boys! Keep to cover."

"To cover yourself, major!" barked George Croghan. "You've been singled out—you've four bullets through your clothes. There'll be a fifth."

Most of the soldiers had crossed the ford, and the Long Knife Americans at last crossed also—facing and firing at the Indians who burst into the road, hot for plunder.

That ended the battle. Doctor Craik was waiting on the other side of the river.

"You're not hurt, colonel?" he asked of Washington.

"No, sir. But I think I'm the only officer on the General's staff unwounded. Two horses were shot from under me."

"I looked to see you killed, a dozen times," exclaimed Doctor Craik. "I hear that the General is wounded. Is that so?"

"Yes, sir; and badly."

"I must go to him at once." Doctor Craik looked at his large, gold watch. "Bless me! Five o'clock! What a bloody day for His Majesty's arms! Who would have thought it! The best troops of Europe defeated by savages and a handful of French!"

"Aye, doctor; and saved from utter destruction by a handful of those whom the General was pleased to term 'backwoodsmen' and 'farmers'" said Washington, a little bitterly. "Would we all had been backwoodsmen, and fought fire with fire. If the Virginians had only been given the advance, as I implored they might—but no matter. If the General survives, next time there will be a different story, for now he knows the value of the American Volunteer."

"Yes," said Doctor Craik; "if there is a next time for him. I fear from the reports that his wound is fatal. He is a brave man. Is it true that he ordered himself to be left—that he wished to stay and die upon the field?"

"I did not hear him say, but Croghan so maintains," said Washington. "I was a little late at the spot where he lay."

So they trudged on, in the rout. Washington walked

slightly staggering, for as plain to be seen and as had been proved by the pillow, he was still not recovered from his sickness.

The Indians did not pursue. They were too busy gathering plunder. That was fortunate. The army had been cut to pieces. Of the fourteen hundred men and officers nearly two-thirds had been killed or wounded, sixty-three out of the eighty-nine officers were dead or disabled and of the three companies of Virginia Rangers only thirty members were unhurt.

This night of July 9, 1755, camp was made upon the other side of the river; but Washington, who was the only aide left to General Braddock, had to ride forty miles upon a wagon horse with rope bridle and without a saddle, through the rain and darkness to find Colonel Dunbar.

The terrible retreat continued. General Braddock died at the Great Meadows, and was buried only about a mile from old Fort Necessity.

Colonel Dunbar was now in command. He took the fragment of the fine army back to Fort Cumberland and refused to lead another attack upon Fort Duquesne. Instead, he decided to go into winter quarters at Philadelphia; so nothing more was to be done this year.

From Fort Cumberland Washington went home to Mount Vernon, to rest. The Hunter was laid up for some time with the arm that had been wounded and should have been attended to earlier. But there were many worse wounds, and the doctors had been busy.

XXI
A Buckskin Corporal

Robert Hunter!

This was his name, now, in the year Seventeen Hundred and Fifty-eight, for he had become a white American and had learned to live as the people of Washington's country lived.

But during the three years since the fight of Braddock's Field things had been going badly for the American frontier. The English soldiers were busy against the French soldiers of Canada. The French and their Indians still held the Ohio; Fort Duquesne had not been marched upon again and after the English had been driven back so easily almost all the Indians had joined the French.

Just why Fort Duquesne was permitted to stand, nobody appeared to know. Scarouady himself had sent word to the Governor of Virginia and to Washington:

"I still have men who will join with you, my brothers, to take up the hatchet again. We do not want the soldiers from across the big water. They are unfit to fight in the woods. Let us go, ourselves; for we came out of this ground and we understand what to do."

Washington had been made commander of all the Virginia soldiers, but it seemed hard work to get men who would leave their homes and march into the woods again. For the Indians of the French were very bold—especially the Delawares and Shawnees. They came across the mountains to attack the Virginia and Maryland border; no one knew where they might strike next; it looked as though northern Virginia was to be put to the hatchet and knife, and a great alarm had seized the town of Winchester, near which, in the Valley of the Shenandoah, old Lord Fairfax lived upon his plantation of Greenway.

And having been working and learning upon this same plantation, under the rule of the queer old lord whom he had first met with Gist and Washington in camp at Will's Creek that night several years back, Robert Hunter also was in the midst of alarms.

Lord Fairfax would not run. He had raised a troop of horse and he had men both white and black, and he said that at his age it didn't matter to him whether he fell by the tomahawk or by sickness.

Washington himself rode into Greenway, and on into Winchester and did his best to quiet the people there. But the trail to Fort Cumberland in the north was watched by the enemy, and a scouting party from Winchester was attacked by French and Indians only twenty miles out and Captain John Mercer and several men killed: so that, as said, it was difficult to get the settlers to leave their homes.

With the skeleton of a regiment, the First Regiment of Virginia Militia, Washington was supposed to guard the long line of the Virginia frontier.

All this trouble would keep up, too, while Fort Duquesne, over there at the Forks of the Ohio, sent its Rangers and Indians against the Americans of the south while the English soldiers were busy in the far north.

At last, in the spring of 1758, it was known that Fort Duquesne was to be taken this very summer. Lord Fairfax got the news as quickly as anybody, for he constantly received letters and papers from England. He liked to talk with Robert, who at eighteen had grown to feel himself a man—and besides, had learned to read and to write and to think white-race thoughts.

Washington rode down from Fort Loudoun, which he had built at Winchester. He and Lord Fairfax, taking Robert (whom Colonel Washington, aged twenty-six, never failed to send for) rode and talked, as in the early days of Greenway Court.

"By George, George!" Lord Fairfax exulted. "They say Forbes, that Scotch doctor, is to lead you into the woods. He won his berth of brigadier in His Majesty's army without favor, and while his record shows him a hard man to turn, you may believe me that he is no Braddock. He's too canny not to look before he leaps. Will you trust your precious carcass to him? Faith, you've been desperately sick; so you might well seize the opportunity of getting as far away from your bed as you can."

"As long as I can move I will join any march to

overthrow Fort Duquesne," answered Washington. "It is a thorn in the side of Virginia, and should have been plucked out long ago. I have repeatedly asked for forces and authority with which to carry the war into the enemy's territory. If we do not do that, this country is lost. There will not be a settler north of the Blue Ridge Mountains. As for Brigadier-General Forbes," Washington added. "I have already, as you might easily guess, applied for a part in the expedition."

"I'll furnish you with one good man, at least," chuckled old Lord Fairfax. "You shall have my half-Indian brave, here, again. Though I don't know who will tell me hunting stories while he is gone."

Washington turned with a brief smile for Robert. He was very thin, and white, for he had indeed been ill. The hardships of the wilderness trail had left their mark upon him.

"Robert the Hunter has been in my mind," he said. "I can count on him as a soldier; and when he joins the colors I shall see that he is made a corporal."

"Ho, ho," Lord Fairfax laughed. "That's an honor. Since poor Braddock's failure with his Regulars I've come to look upon a corporal of your 'raw Provincials' as rather more dependable than a red-coat sergeant. But mark my words, George: you'll find John Forbes a different kind of man."

There were to be two regiments from Virginia, three from Pennsylvania, several companies from Maryland, two from North Carolina; a battalion of Royal Americans who were King's soldiers under Regular officers; and a regiment of Highlanders who were Scotch Regulars sent from across the water.

"By George, when the claymore meets the tomahawk— eh, George?" had chuckled Lord Fairfax. "And which'll be the more astonished, think you: The wild Hielander when he sees a man wi' no skeen on his head (for they don't scalp in Scotland) or the wild Injun when he sees a bonny warrior in petticoats?"

The whole force numbered about six thousand men. Six or seven hundred Catawbas and Cherokees were expected. Brigadier-General John Forbes, a hard fighter and a veteran, was in Philadelphia, to take command. Washington had been gladly accepted to command the Long Knife Americans. If anybody knew about Fort Duquesne, he did. It looked as though Fort Duquesne would be taken this time; especially when word came that many of its Indians had gone home, rich with plunder, and that the garrison was small.

And the English were beginning to gain victories in the north, which so frightened the Ohio Indians that they commenced to exchange peace belts with the Governor of Pennsylvania. Even Shingis was "willing."

The march, however, was delayed, as usual. Washington advised General Forbes to take the Braddock road, which needed only a little repairing. But General Forbes (who seemed to have ideas of his own) decided to make a new road from central Pennsylvania straight to Fort Duquesne. People told him that the mountains were lower and the rivers less swift.

If he had listened to Washington he would have got to Duquesne sooner and with much less trouble. But Washington had his way in one thing: he put two hundred of his men into hunter clothes of buckskin shirt and leggins, and blankets, and sent them forward under Major Andrew Lewis to Colonel Henry Bouquet of the Royal Americans, who commanded at the rendezvous camp while General Forbes lay sick in Philadelphia.

It seemed good to Robert Hunter to be in buckskin; and all the men (and Washington also) were pleased when Colonel Bouquet the Regular said that this was the most proper dress he had seen yet.

Colonel Bouquet's camp was at Raystown, of central Pennsylvania north from Fort Cumberland. While the road was being cut ahead, he built a fort named Fort Bedford (which became the town of Bedford, Pennsylvania); he had the Highlanders—who were a strange sight in their things called "kilts" that did look like short petticoats, and the Royal Americans in dark red coats faced with blue, and part of the Virginians (among them Robert) in hunting shirts and in green uniforms faced with buff.

When the road had been hacked out far enough (a terrible road that had proved to be, too; much worse than the Washington and Braddock road) he marched forty miles across the Alleghany Mountains to Loyalhannon Creek on the other side of the same Laurel Hills crossed farther west by the Washington and Braddock road.

Washington had been at Fort Cumberland, completing his regiments; but he would follow. He had not missed the Braddock fight, and he certainly would not miss this. General Forbes was still very sick in Philadelphia—and working from his bed; but he would be on hand, too.

At Loyalhannon Creek Colonel Bouquet began another supply fort. This was General Forbes' plan: not to bore in as General Braddock had done, with a lot of baggage to guard; but to leave bases, as he went, for his supplies; and when he was near Duquesne to use all his men and take it quickly.

Now this was already September, and the rains had fallen and the road had been the worst that even Robert had yet seen. The Catawbas and Cherokees had been no good at all— why, one Mingo such as Scarouady was worth a hundred of them. They did go out, a few, under Long Knife officers, and brought in news and scalps; but as a rule, they could not be believed. They even stole some of the scalps, and pretended that they had taken them. Therefore, just what the garrison at Fort Duquesne were doing nobody knew; nor how many they were.

But it was known that they did not number a great many, and that the Indians were leaving them.

Now Fort Duquesne was about fifty miles away. Major James Grant of the Highlanders, it was said, had been wishing to go on and have a look at the fort, perhaps capture some of its men in the woods and bring them back.

Colonel Bouquet finally consented. So Grant took part of his Highlanders, and part of the Royal Americans, and the Major Lewis Buckskins, and some of the Pennsylvanians and the Maryland companies.

That turned out to be a bad move. How Robert himself ever got out alive he hardly knew. For when they all had arrived in the dark of early morning on top of the hill (the same hill!) less than a mile from the fort, Major Grant sent the Virginians down to draw out the fort's Indians and lead them back into an ambush.

Major Andrew Lewis was an old Indian fighter, but he did not relish this job. A thick fog had settled, making the darkness worse. Nobody had any idea what lay before, down there in the cleared ground where the French Indians were supposed to be camped.

All that he could do was to send scouts ahead to feel the way while he tried to follow. So once again Robert the Hunter found himself stealing forward to spy upon the enemy at Fort Duquesne.

This was blind work! Very soon he had lost the other scouts and the fort too. He could see nothing, nothing; and he blundered on, while the dense forest dripped with the fog. Then, when he was putting one hand before the other, and groping from trunk to trunk, and log to log, as he crawled, and had heard no sound of Indians his fingers fell upon a new, a fearsome object. It was fuzzily smooth, and dank, and ridged——

Ugh! It was a shaven head!

U-u-ugh! Over backward he went, with the Indian on top of him, weighting him down and clutching at his throat, and growling angrily.

The growls were in a language that he knew.

"Hold! Scarouady!" he managed to gasp. "You know me."

Scarouady let up.

"Ho, ho! The Hunter! What do you do here, crawling without eyes?"

"I scout for the Long Knives. What do you do, hiding in the bushes?"

"I scout, too," said Scarouady. "But I wait for eyes. Where are your Long Knives?"

That, Robert did not know. He explained; whereat Scarouady grunted.

"I have seen those petticoat warriors. Is the captain who commands used to the woods?"

Robert thought not.

"I sent word to Washington and Assaragoa that I would help fight the French if those soldiers from across the water did not interfere," said Scarouady. "And now here are across-the-water soldiers in petticoats like women, come to the woods. Wah! The English are crazy. Why isn't Washington sent in, with his men who understand?"

Washington was coming, Robert explained; and so was a red-coat General who would listen to reason, and was brave besides.

"He is Head of Iron," approved Scarouady. "I have heard of him. Very well. But he can do nothing without Washington. And now you and I can do nothing. It is better to sit still and wait than to walk into the enemy."

They waited. The woods paled, but the fog hung low and shut them in. Then, after a long wait, with the fog beginning to thin a little, first they smelled smoke, as if they might be near an Indian camp. Then, when the fog had thinned more, they could just see a house burning, to their right, in the cleared ground before the fort.

The house was between them and the hill that Robert had left; he had had no idea that he was so far in. Then, with the fog lifting rapidly, down out of it marched a company of soldiers, right into the cleared ground.

Now a cluster of Indian lodges could be seen close against the fort walls; the burning building was a fort storehouse; and the company of soldiers were Highlanders.

Where were the Major Lewis Buckskins? Had they got lost, too? Just what to do, Robert did not know. But Scarouady grunted.

"The petticoat warriors are fools, like the red-coats. You and I will stay out of this, for I see trouble."

The Highland men had halted within cannon shot of the fort and several of them seemed to be making a map! The Indians at the fort were pointing, for the air was now bright. And then, from the hill, drums beat the reveille, as if daring the fort people to come out!

"Ugh!" uttered Scarouady. "Look! They wake up!"

For, drowning the drum roll, the fort Indians had answered with the war-whoop; and out of the fort gates were rushing the French—some of them in only their shirts, but all armed; and they and the Indians, numbering hundreds, charged for the Highland company.

"Wah!" cried Scarouady. "The petticoat warriors mean to fight."

And they did fight. They stood firmly, their guns belched, the French and Indians broke, and flowed on either side; the Highland men turned about, they charged through, their captain fell dead, but they got into the woods, and next the woods were full of shooting and yelling. Indians were running in every direction.

"We shall have to get out of here," said Scarouady. He and Robert ran.

They ran a long distance, dodging the shooting, for it was a question of saving their scalps. The woods were like a hornets' nest. After about two miles they discovered more men.

"Long Knives!" Scarouady cried; and with Robert shouting "Friend!" they ran in to these.

These were Captain Bullitt's company, guarding the baggage on the trail. They were anxious and peering, for they had heard the battle sounds; but Robert had had scarcely time to gasp the news when the woods echoed more loudly, and the Highland soldiers began to race in.

"What's the word? Quick?" Captain Bullitt demanded.

"A' beaten, a' beaten!" they wailed. "We ha' seen gude men up to their hunkers in mud an' a' the skeen aff their heads!"

"Where is Major Lewis, corporal?" Captain Bullitt shouted to Robert.

"I don't know, sir. I was sent on a scout early in the morning."

"He was afterward ordered back here to the baggage so as to give the Regulars the glory!" stormed Captain Bullitt. "Now he's gone on his own hook to help the Regulars! Well, they didn't want the Buckskins, but they'll be glad of 'em now! Quick, men! We'll fort behind the baggage and save what men we can. We'll not run from the red rascals."

In a moment the rout poured in, with the Indians and the French close behind. Aye, but that was a fight! The fifty "backwoodsmen" of Captain Bullitt gave ball for ball. The war-whoop of Scarouady sounded high; the musket in Robert the Hunter's hands grew hot.

They were savage, those Indians who usually feared the Long Knives; and the French mingled with them. At last Captain Bullitt waited until they had crowded to within thirty feet; then he gave the word: "Fire!" The muskets spoke together, mowing down the enemy. "With the bayonet: Charge!" That cleared the field.

The wagons were loaded at lightning speed, the wounded were put aboard, no more fugitives were coming in; and they all hastened back for Loyalhannon.

It was learned later that Major Grant and Major Lewis had both been captured. Major Lewis (a strapping man, very strong) had killed a warrior in hand-to-hand fight before he surrendered.

Altogether Major Grant had lost two hundred and seventy-three out of eight hundred; and of the "Provincials" Captain Bullitt was the only officer unhurt.

XXII
The Fall Of The Great Fort

After this there was no doubt as to the value of the American "Provincials," whether in buckskin or in rags. The Major Lewis battalion had held the enemy while the Major Grant Regulars had retreated; and then Captain Bullitt's company had saved these, or they would all have been killed in the woods.

General Forbes issued an order complimenting Washington upon his men, and Captain Bullitt was promoted to be a major.

As for Robert, he had been lucky; and as for Scarouady, he went away, disgusted again with the foolishness of fighting with one's eyes closed.

The useless battle in front of Fort Duquesne had occurred about the middle of September. October passed, with Colonel Bouquet waiting here at Loyalhannon where he had finished the supply-fort named Fort Ligonier.

Washington was bringing on the new Virginia regiment, and General Forbes was on the way from his sick bed.

Washington arrived first. If ever a man was welcome, it was he. The very sight of him gave confidence that the onward march would be made with sense.

But General Forbes was coming on from Raystown in a litter, with the main column. The fifty miles of new road had been found to be very bad, and Fort Duquesne was another fifty miles ahead. November had opened with rain and snow again; the Virginia and Maryland troops were short of clothing and blankets. If fifty days had been spent in getting this far, only fifty miles, when could they all break through the next fifty miles upon a winter trail?

General Forbes arrived in his litter. A council of war was held; and in that even Washington advised that nothing more be done until spring. 'Twas plain to be seen how disappointed he was. All the Virginians knew that if his first advice had been taken, and the march had been made over his and Braddock's road, through country that had been mapped and explored many a time, before this the army would have been comfortable in Duquesne.

But a lucky thing happened. Since the Major Grant battle the French and Indians had been bolder, and had prowled around Loyalhannon, firing by night on the sentries. One night, after Washington came—in fact, the very night after the council, a trap was set by an advance outpost, with Robert himself in charge.

By tracks that had been found, the enemy stole up under cover of a high bank along the creek and hid there to pick off the sentries. Very good! With his little squad Corporal Hunter crouched in the brush above the bank, and waited. Early in the morning the enemy came—six, led by a French officer.

"Fire!" Corporal Hunter suddenly ordered; the muskets flared through the dimness, and the men charged out. The enemy ran like shadows flitting. There were two dead Indians, but Robert did not pause for these. He had his eye upon the Frenchman. The Frenchman had been wounded in the leg; and when he found he could not get away he turned about and cried: "Mercy! Mercy!"

So Robert marched him to the fort.

This was a valuable capture. It might mean the fall of Fort Duquesne. Huzzah, huzzah! The Frenchman said that an officer named Ligneris commanded Fort Duquesne. The English armies in the north had cut off his provisions. His men were leaving him. Even his Indians were going home; the Delawares, Shawnees and Mingos had refused to help the French any longer, for they feared the wrath of the Long Knives; the Potawatomis and Ottawas and Hurons were tired of war—they said that now the English had been stopped, and they wished to go home for the winter. Fort Duquesne had only five or six hundred men.

Whether or not the Frenchman was lying, this put new life into the army. Snow, rain, mud and hunger mattered no longer; the time to strike had arrived; and Washington's worn face brightened.

He and his Virginians and the Pennsylvanians were to be given the advance at last; stripped of baggage, taking only their knapsacks and blankets, twenty-five hundred picked men were to press after. That was the Washington way.

Washington commanded but Colonel George Armstrong commanded the Pennsylvanians. Now the road onward had to be made in the rain and the snow and the mud. Sometimes the Pennsylvanians took the lead, and sometimes the Virginians; but with Washington encouraging, always calm, always strong, never disheartened, the Virginians finally got ahead and stayed there.

A fire-place was ordered by him, at each supply camp, to warm the General; for old Iron Head was coming in his litter. He was a man! And when the Potawatomis, Ottawas, Hurons and other of the Lake Indians at the fort learned from spies that the Long Knives of Washington were making the road, they refused to attack them. They had had experience with these soldiers who fought with their eyes open and rarely missed.

Six or seven miles of road were all that could be hewed out in a day. It was November 24 when the road was within six miles of the fort; and halt had been made until the main column came in, with Head of Iron borne in his curtained litter. And here was Scarouady, bringing Aroas, White Thunder, and other Mingos to greet Washington.

"Wah!" Scarouady said to Robert. "Is it true that Head of Iron is carried in that thing to keep him safe?"

"Yes," said Robert.

"We have come to see," continued Scarouady. "For the French Indians are told he is a man of such terrible temper that he must be guarded on the march or he will run wild and spread death among all the Indians who would fight him."

"That is true," answered Robert.

"Well," said Scarouady, "I think Washington is going to take the fort, unless more foolishness is done. We will wait on the hill and see, for we have risked our lives before and gained nothing."

The General was so weak from his pain that the officers urged him to wait a day or two before making the attack.

"No," he replied. "I will sleep in Fort Duquesne tomorrow night or I will sleep nowhere."

There had been smoke, this evening, in the direction of the fort; and in the middle of the night a great "Boom!" shook the woods. What this meant nobody knew and nobody cared.

They all would see on the morrow.

In the morning they started on from these headwaters of Turkey Creek, near whose mouth, not many miles west, General Braddock's army had been cut to pieces.

The day was dark and chill—this day when Fort Duquesne should fall, after four years of defiance.

The Buckskins led, to clear the road of the enemy. After them followed Head of Iron, in his litter, at the fore of the Highlanders. The Royal Americans held the right, under Colonel Bouquet. The other Virginians, and the Pennsylvanians and the Maryland and North Carolina companies held the left, under Washington. The drums beat—tap, tap—and the steady tramp of feet rustled the dead leaves of the forest aisles.

About noon they all began to pass skeletons; those were the remains of men killed during the Grant battle two months back.

From the scout-line Robert now and again could see these three columns toiling on through the wet, naked woods, up hill and down. The scouts had sighted no enemy, yet.

In the early dusk the view of the Forks opened from around Grant's Hill. What was that? See! The fort was afire— the walls were smouldering under a canopy of smoke, and beyond, in the Ohio, the last of a fleet of boats was disappearing in the mists! Huzzah! The scouts ran boldly through the clearing; and stopped short. Wah!

Robert found himself at a race-track used by the Indians for foot-races. It stretched straight-away, and was marked by poles set upon either side of it; and every pole was topped by the head of a Highlander with his petticoat clothing hung beneath!

An Indian joke! Whew! Now what would happen? The scouts did not have long to wait. Down among the stumps marched the Washington Buckskins; they had won the honor of the lead, and Washington rode at their front. The Pennsylvanians and the other Provincials followed closely. One and all they saw the heads upon the poles, but this did not stop them. The Royal Americans in their red and blue came next, their fifes and drums playing merrily. The Highlanders strode after, with Head of Iron in his litter leading them on.

What now? Listen! They had sighted the first of the heads—they had broken into a hoarse growl. The growl spread; and see! They had gone mad! They had thrown away their muskets, they had bared their stout swords, they were coming in a mob, like wild buffalo; their bare knees worked up and down, their kilt petticoats flapped, the ribbons of their caps streamed behind them, and treading under foot whatever was in their path they charged for the fort, to kill.

But there was nobody in the fort. The French had blown up the ammunition magazine (this had been the "Boom!" in the night), and had gone away in boats.

"The last boats left only an hour before the Long Knives came," said Scarouady. "Well, now Washington and I have been at the death of this great house which the English should have taken years ago. It was a house of much mischief."

That was a moment not to be forgotten, when, with all the troops presenting arms, and the fifes piping and shrilling, and the drums rolling, by order of General Forbes himself Colonel George Washington, the youngest field officer, raised the flag over the ruins of Fort Duquesne. He had earned that honor.

The Ohio country was to be English; the French had made a strong fight, but they never were to come back.

"Your reports upon this place are correct, Colonel Washington," said the worn old Head of Iron. "It is the site for a fort, and the site for a city. In the name of His Majesty I christen it Pittsburgh, as a tribute to Sir William Pitt, His Majesty's great prime minister who has so vigorously prosecuted this war to the glory of His Majesty's arms."

Huzzah, huzzah, huzzah!

XXIII
Colonel Washington Rests

The next day was spent in resting. Little was left of Fort Duquesne save the charred logs of the palisades, and the tall chimneys of the buildings.

Several more Indians came in. They were Delawares and Shawnees, who wished to see Head of Iron—that terrible chief who had to be guarded in a litter, lest he break loose and spread death. They were anxious to look upon Washington again, who was under the protection of the Great Spirit.

Thirteen fair shots had been made at him in the Braddock fight, by a chief. Not one bullet had struck him. Evidently he was not to be slain by bullets.

While quarters were being built for the new garrison the bones of the Grant soldiers were gathered and buried. Then a number of the soldiers wished to see Braddock's Field. So they went out, with Robert and others of the Virginians who had seen it before.

The Delawares and Shawnees acted as guides. As for Robert, there had been such a rout and excitement that he had had time to note very little. How long ago that seemed!

The woods from the ambush hill to the river were still strewn with skeletons—the tree trunks were scarred with bullets and cannon-balls, and fragments of clothing, grenadier hats and rusted muskets were scattered everywhere.

Young Major Peter Halket, of General Forbes' staff, wondered if anybody could tell him where his father and younger brother had fallen. Robert asked the Shawnees—"Two red-coat soldiers," he said: "an old gray-haired man and a boy. They fell together, the boy on top of his father, down toward the river." He remembered that.

"Ho!" cried one of the Shawnees. "Yes; I saw. It was many moons ago, but I will try to find the spot."

He led off, and they all followed. And after a time he stopped, to peer about. Then he ran straight; then they heard him cry, from the woods—a discovery whoop. Then they went in to him. He was waiting under an oak tree. He pointed at the foot of it, where leaves were heaped up.

Captain West, who commanded the party, formed a circle of the men and ordered the leaves to be raked aside. And sure enough, here were two skeletons, one with its arms around the other. They were old Major Halket, the brave Scotch nobleman, and his son. Young Major Halket knew by the teeth which had been his father's.

The bones were wrapped in a Highland plaid, and buried, and a volley fired over the grave.

The quarters having been built, and two hundred Virginians under Lieutenant Colonel Hugh Mercer having been detailed to guard them, the column started home. It was the middle of December when the Virginians were finally in Fort Loudoun of Winchester. They were to be disbanded. In Washington's opinion they had served enough; a "really fine corps" General Forbes had called them; now the border was clean of the enemy, and it was time that they be mustered out.

Washington resigned his post of commander—which made the men all the more anxious to quit soldiering and go home, too. The two regiments drew up an address to him—

"In you we place the most implicit confidence," it said. "Your presence only will cause a steady firmness and vigor to actuate every breast, despising the greatest dangers, and thinking light of toils and hardships, while led on by the man we know and love."

This was the Thirtieth Day of December, 1758. He handed in his commission very soon; and on January 6 he was married. That had not been unexpected. He had been sending out letters to Mrs. Martha Custis, from every camp; and he had been in a great hurry to get back, after the capture of the fort.

The English were growing stronger, the French were growing weaker. The Seven Years War between Great Britain and France lasted about five years longer; France lost not only the Ohio Country but Canada as well; Onontio of the Indians was driven from America.

But in this fighting Robert Hunter and the other Buckskins took no part. They had to wait for a greater war, when Washington again proved his mettle and his wisdom.

That, however, was still years ahead; although, said certain people, among them old Lord Fairfax, it was surely coming.

THE END

www.ingramcontent.com/pod-product-compliance
Lightning Source LLC
Chambersburg PA
CBHW020330160726
47992CB00004B/1774